Fret Sawing *For* Pleasure *And* Profit

Published by
Henry T. Williams
New York
1877

The Toolemera Press
History Preserved
www.toolemerapress.com

Fret Sawing For Pleasure And Profit
Published by Henry T. Williams
New York
1877

No part of this book may be reproduced, stored in an electronic retrieval system, or transmitted in any form or by an means, electronic, mechanical, photocopy, photographic or otherwise without the written permission of the publisher.

Excerpts of one page or less for the purposes of review and comment are permissible.

Copyright © 2019 Gary Roberts, DBA, The Toolemera Press
All rights reserved.

International Standard Book Number
ISBN : 978-1-0878-0949-6
(Trade Paperback)

Published by
The Toolemera Press
Wilmington, North Carolina
USA 28401

www.toolemerapress.com

Manufactured in the United States of America.

19th century historical context of *Fret-Sawing For Pleasure And Profit.*

by Gary Roberts, Publisher, The Toolemera Press

Demorest's Family Magazine, Volume 14, 1878. *"How To Use The Fret Saw." - The name of Henry T. Williams is becoming synonymous as a publisher with works descriptive of the modern minor arts and artistic industries. His latest publication of this kind, "Fret-Sawing For Pleasure And Profit," is like those which have preceded it, a most excellent manual of the particular art which it pictures and describes. Beginning with a chapter devoted to materials and implements, it tells all about the proper kinds of wood to be used in Fret Sawing, their qualities and peculiarities. It gives illustrations and diagrams of tools and presses, furnishes a quantity of beautiful designs, and teaches how to gild, dye and stain wood to produce picturesque effects. There is also a chapter upon hand-carving, and easy directions for inlaying and over-laying, in addition to many useful suggestions in regard to the adaptability of material and design to work. To amateurs and lovers of this beautiful work, it will prove an invaluable auxiliary, and we strongly recommend it to their consideration.*

The emergence of an affluent merchant class took place during the second half of the 19th century in America, Great Britain and in various parts of Europe. To have free time for activities of leisure became an expression of both monetary and social success as opposed to the working class activities of tradesmen, farmers, local shop keepers, etc. At the same time, ecumenical influence encouraged "Hands To Work, Hearts To God", as opined by the Shaker community, more properly known as The United Society of Believers in Christ's Second Appearing.

Yet, doing craftwork that produced vernacular objects was considered to be neither proper nor acceptable for young men and women, much less adults. The phrase "the minor arts" was coined to describe the production of objects of beauty that would enhance the home while not stooping to the level of the local tradesman. The minor arts included woodcraft, pottery, painting, paperwork, decorating textiles, etc. To be capable of using your hands to make an object of beauty was to be admired by your neighbors. To do so also indicated to your neighbors that you had leisure time to spare, that although of the middle class, your success was such that you could allow time for yourself, your wife or your children to practice the minor arts.

In the United States Of America, yet undergoing the growing pains of the industrial revolution, the suggestion arose amongst middle class society that the average man, and rarely the average woman, could augment their earned income through minor arts activities. This became a selling point for authors, publishers and the often itinerant book dealers who visited towns to ply their wares to both the citizenry and to the local stationer. Get Rich Quick was a common denominator in this genre of books. Unlike the books of this type published in Great Britain which focused solely on craft as a socially acceptable activity, many of those issued by American publishers featured the carrot-on-a-stick motive of profit.

Wood carving and fret-work were amongst the most popular leisure activities of the time period. While wood carving required both skill and training in order to produce an acceptable object, basic fret-work could be produced with minimal tools using either readily available commercial patterns or from original patterns. An attractive and ornamental object that might or might not serve a purpose was well within the skills of the average person. Combining ornamental fret-work with basic carpentry skills, attractive items such as display shelves and desk accessories could be produced that contributed to the social standing of the home. The frequency of fret-work patterns incorporating Christian themes furthered the acceptance of the craft as an acceptable past time.

A variety of youth's serials of this time period featured writings intended to direct the young man, and on occasion the young woman, towards manual pursuits that would occupy their free time, thus preventing them from straying towards perfidy and licentious behaviors. 1866 saw the publication of *Our Workshop*, by Temple Thorold, the first distinct book to introduce woodcraft as an acceptable leisure time activity. James Lukin, active in the Church Of England, was a prolific author of 19th century books on a variety of crafts and minor arts, again for the benefit of the emotional and religious development of the individual. David Denning, yet another popular author of the time period, focused on more advanced aspects of craft for the amateur, aka, the non-tradesman.

To this genre we owe the preservation of period craft techniques that might otherwise have disappeared or saved only in first person oral and anecdotal histories.

Gary Roberts, publisher of The Toolemera Press, re-publishes classic books on early crafts, trades and industries, from his personal library.

History Preserved
www.toolemera.com

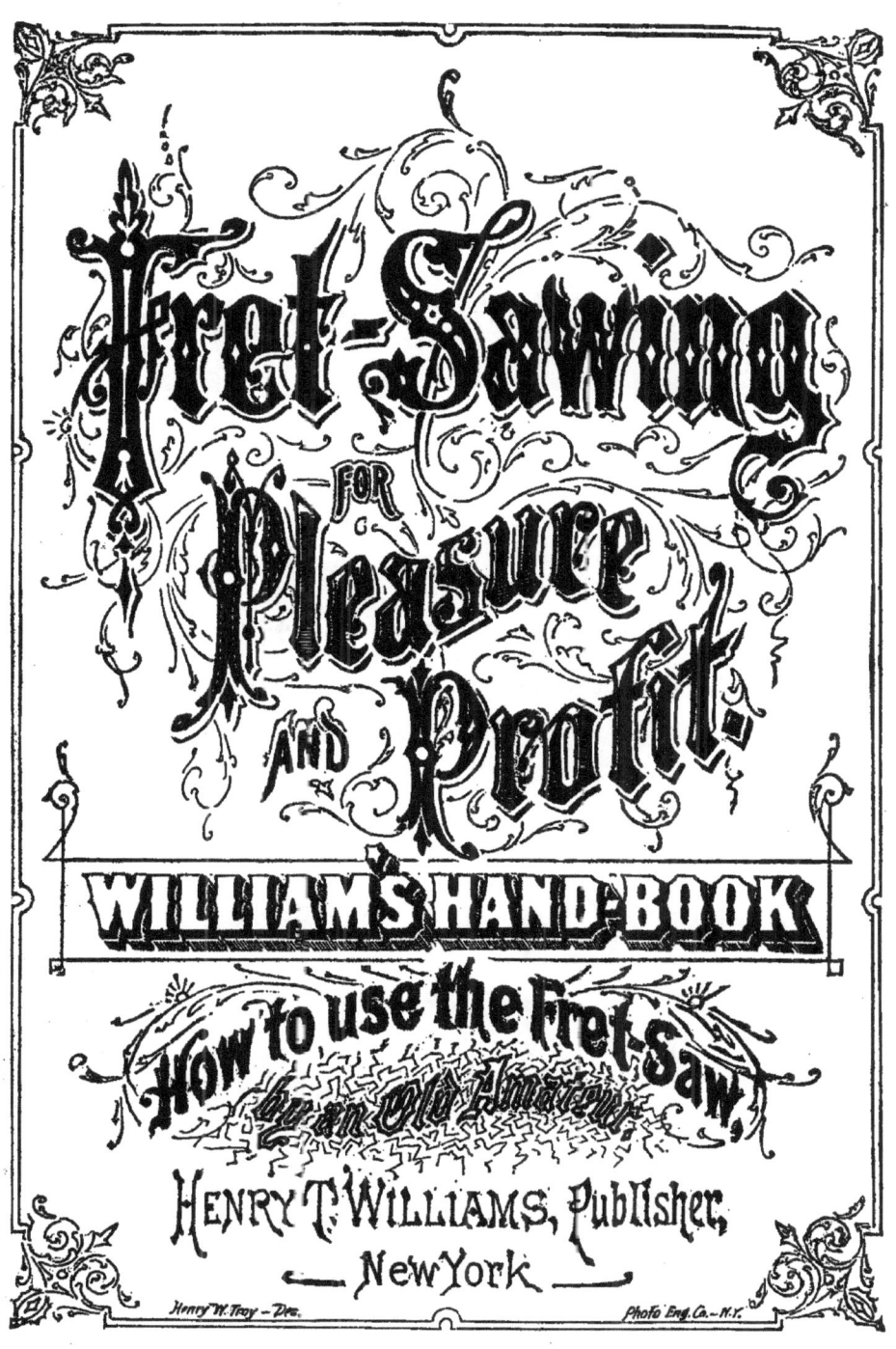

PRICE 50 CENTS.

Entered according to Act of Congress, in the year 1877, by
HENRY T. WILLIAMS,
in the office of the Librarian of Congress, at Washington, D. C.

BRADSTREET PRESS,
279, 281 AND 283 BROADWAY,
NEW YORK.

TO THE

Inventive Genius of America,

THAT HAS SOUGHT OUT MANY WAYS TO ALLEVIATE MERE LABOR, BY THE
ALLIANCE OF PLEASURE TO PROFIT, MAKING THE HEART
A COADJUTOR OF THE HAND AND BRAIN,

THIS VOLUME IS INSCRIBED.

Design for Picture Frame.

INTRODUCTION.

IDLE HOURS, through the resources of Art, are rendered less tedious and burdensome; yet *Amateur Art* must by no means be classed among the time-killing occupations of the day, nor is it a source of amusement alone, for it combines the useful with the ornamental. There is no need of idle hours. Man was created to be busy, and to appreciate the exercise of thought, talent, ingenuity, and when labor joins hands with symmetry and beauty, we render it homage under the name of Art, as in distinction from mere Work.

Fret-sawing has taken a strong hold upon the affections of our people, and, although of recent introduction, it comes to us with a fixed responsibility to plain natural laws that have an antiquity equal to the universe itself. Those laws cannot change, and their operation is the same in a steam-engine as in a watch.

Under such conditions we propose to discuss the subject of fret-sawing, and *not as a toy*. Already much has been said of it, but we modestly imagine that at least a portion of this book may serve to extend the knowledge of such hints as have been gained from practical experience, which is the most thorough teacher. And we feel that for such knowledge there is a need. The youngsters have won high encomiums from doting relations over match-boxes, brackets and other knick-knacks, that seemed difficult enough to accomplish even without much respect for straight lines and proper proportions. Practice has pointed out defects, and, these being remedied, the march is still onward towards greater efforts and more wonderful results. Like Oliver Twist, the fret-sawyers are crying for "more," and if the information herein given, as the result of effort which has felt the same craving for a more intimate acquaintance with Art, can minister to this need, then we shall not have written this book in vain.

Cherish a love for the beautiful; it is a sentiment pure and good. True Art will offer nothing degrading to an honest mind, while the contrast of symbolism will oftentimes lead us to look for a counterpart in the character of ourselves and those around us, that it may be known if we, too, are faithful specimens of the Master's work.

CHAPTER I.

OF MATERIALS.

The substances that may be wrought into beautiful and useful articles by the aid of the fret-saw, are many and various. Gold, silver, copper, iron, and, in fact, any metal which is not as hard as the saw-blade itself, can easily be cut, as also all kinds of woods, ivory, bone, and such like material.

Now if you will take a bit of metal and examine it through a magnifying glass, you will discover that the fibre is much finer and closer than that of the other substances mentioned. This peculiarity denotes a greater degree of friction when brought under the action of the saw-blade; therefore a different speed must be given to the saw, and the mechanic must remember to equalize that friction by a lower rate of speed than that required for wood, since all extra velocity increases the friction which it is desirable to overcome. We shall probably find a more fitting chapter to enlarge upon this point ere we come to the finis.

The most common material for the amateur's use is wood, some suitable sorts of which we will describe, as forming two classes.

Under the first class we will place the soft woods and such as are of secondary use—pine, Spanish cedar (which, by the way, is not a cedar at all), butternut, red cedar (also a misnomer, it being a species of juniper), ordinary white juniper (cupressus thyoides), poplar, white-wood (liriodendron), and bass-wood.

PINE.

Pine is too well known to tax your patience with a description of the more common variety (white), or even of the resinous pitch pine. The former may be found useful for linings, bottoms of boxes, and all such purposes where it cannot show its cheapness, as for the foundation of veneered work, though for that mahogany is far preferable. The Southern pine is finely marked, and really handsome, though the resin it contains will tax your patience; yet we have seen handsome work done in this wood.

SPANISH CEDAR.

Spanish Cedar is easily obtained from second-hand cigar boxes. It is a miserable wood for fret-sawing, coarse in fibre, and, though it can readily be stained, it does not take either oil or polish well, on account of its being very porous. By reason of its odor it might be agreeable to some for lining boxes, and it has one of the virtues of mahogany, in not being liable to warp. We should not recommend it as a standard fine wood, or, indeed, for any but coarse or rudimental work. Nice workmanship deserves better material. Understand, however, that we do not utterly condemn it, but wish to fix the idea that finer woods are more attractive and suitable for general purposes, and are quoted at the same, if not less, price.

BUTTERNUT.

Butternut, otherwise called white walnut, which is its true name, for it belongs to the species Juglans, is a pretty wood, but soft. It cuts clean, and is adapted for a variety of work, *not delicate in design*. It has the same grain as black walnut, and is one of the most common woods of North America. It stains well, shows oiling to advantage, and is a firmer, harder grained wood than either red cedar or white juniper, which we proceed to describe.

CEDAR—JUNIPER.

Red Cedar and *White Juniper* hardly differ, except in color. The former is undoubtedly more handsomely marked, and, being a scarcer wood, brings a higher price. It takes a beautiful polish, which brings out the natural hues, though they fade rapidly. Both of these woods are pitchy, and, therefore, difficult to cut, requiring careful handling, lest they split and break, which, according to the universal depravity of inanimate things, they will do upon the least provocation.

POPLAR.

Poplar is a white, soft, light wood, not liable to shrink, warp or swell. There are several varieties, but the white will, no doubt, be found useful for sundry purposes of the fret-sawyer, such as back-grounds, linings and veneered work. The most particular use made of this wood is in the manufacture of wooden tooth-picks, now to be found in every restaurant.

WHITE-WOOD.

White-wood, the American tulip tree, is rather yellow than white. It is a cheap wood, used largely by cabinet-makers for linings of drawers, shelves, and where it is kept out of sight, lest its plebeian appearance vex critical eyes. It is straight in grain, and free from knots, easily worked. The amateur will find it well adapted for some work to be afterward described.

BASS-WOOD

Bass-wood is another common American variety, furnished by the linden or lime tree. It is a soft, whitish wood, but tough and durable, and much used by turners and carvers.

In the *second* class we will enumerate the highly ornamental and valuable woods, worth the expense of skillful labor, and satisfactory in results.

BLACK WALNUT.

The most common of these is *Black Walnut*, a wood that has almost supplanted mahogany and rosewood, and is, in its own turn, becoming more costly than in former times. The many different markings of this wood baffle description. It is coarse, it is fine; it is straight in grain, it is wavy and mottled; it is all of one shade, and it is streaked; in some sections it grows soft, and in others it is hard. A material which is so variable can therefore serve many uses, and the amateur must use judgment in his selection. We have often found it profitable to purchase handsome specimens whenever convenient and to be procured, with a view to future use in particular kinds of work, for finely marked black walnut is not always to be had for the asking. This wood will take a beautiful polish, and is susceptible of more variations in that respect than many others, and still look well. Plain oiling seems to harden the fibre, and a dead polish will often show better in the work than though it shone like a mirror. Good black walnut ought never to be varnished, for it gives a common look to the article, and fails to bring out the grain. This wood has become much more in demand since the introduction of fret-sawing in this country, though it is now quite as commonly used as pine. In some sections the supply of the growing timber has been entirely exhausted, and though we have often heard predictions of its utter disappearance, there are large forests of it yet in the mountain regions of the Southern States and other parts of the Union, quite adequate for all the demands of many years to come. A variety grown in Kentucky is quite as finely marked as any of that styled French black walnut, so well known from its use in first-class cabinet work. Unless well seasoned by kiln-drying or other process, it will warp and split with the utmost readiness. This bad habit can be remedied in most cases, as we shall learn in a subsequent chapter.

WHITE HOLLY.

White Holly is also a wood that has become very popular. It is very clean and fine grained, closer in texture than any other of our native woods, and does not readily absorb foreign matter, being pure white, more so than the generality of ivory, and quite tough. The whiteness is due to a particular mode of seasoning, and subsequent exposure gives it a mellow creamy tint that is not unpleasing in some respects. A coating of bleached shellac will protect it, but it must be remembered that a shiny apppearance helps to destroy the effect in almost all cases. Very often dingy holly may be easily cleaned with a bit of chamois leather, dipped into clean dry Paris white; and also, as the wood is of such close grain, a *careful* rubbing with very fine sand-paper will prove efficacious. Nothing short of a planing-machine will easily render this wood smooth of surface, and only extra care in seasoning and subsequent storing in a dry place will prevent it from warping and splitting.

EBONY.

Ebony is in direct contrast to holly, being coal black; that is, the ebony which we are familiar with, for there is a greenish-brown variety found in the West Indies, the species found in Ceylon and India, which has a black ground beautifully striped with rich yellowish brown, and the exceedingly rare Calamander wood, with its delicate fawn-colored ground, over which is disposed graceful dark wavings and blotches, almost black. There is sometimes offered for ebony, which indeed it much resembles, a black wood from an Abyssinian tree called Mozzungha, but it belongs to an entirely different order than ebony.

Sawing ebony will prove untidy work, as the dust will blacken everything it may happen to be rubbed upon; but it cuts clear and fine as horn, and quite as hard. It is not very elastic, rather inclined to break than bend, and its fine close grain admits of a magnificent polish, or even oiling. As it is seldom more than six inches wide, only small articles can be made of it in one piece, though, to compensate for that, it is the best wood of all for trinkets, small crosses, charms, bracelets and such like braveries worn by womankind. Ebony can be made smooth with a cabinet scraper, a cheap useful tool of which we shall speak anon, though a good planing-machine will shave it down with less labor and expense of patience. It is a costly wood, but well repays careful work, and is just the right color to keep clean. For marquetry its use is highly essential, and it does not warp very readily, though changes of temperature will sometimes cause it to check and split.

MAHOGANY.

Mahogany is an excellent wood to cut. It turns dark with age, takes a splendid polish, and holds glue the best of all woods. It is too well known to describe.

ROSEWOOD.

Rosewood is the name given to the wood of a number of different trees, and the botanists are still doubtful where to place it. The variety we use is brought from South America. It is a handsome wood, often elegantly marked, will polish like glass, but containing much resinous gum, it is difficult to saw, an obstacle which may be readily overcome by oiling the saw-blade slightly, to lessen the friction, as we shall learn under the appropriate heading. The gum keeps it from warping much.

There is one variety of rosewood growing in Africa of which the writer obtained a small supply. It is beautifully marked, having the color of black walnut, hard in texture, but free from resinous gum, with all the other qualities of our rosewood. The odor of these woods when being sawed is quite perceptible, more than agreeable, we think, though, by a stretch of imagination, it is compared to the perfume of a rose.

SATINWOOD.

Satinwood, which seems to be very properly named, belongs to the same botanical species as mahogany. Some specimens are fine and soft as satin, and its yellowish tint has a natural gloss that is not unpleasing without further polish. The perfume of this wood is quite agreeable, though it is said to be poisonous in large quantities. The reader need not be deterred on that account, however, as the little he would use could have no dangerous effect whatsoever. It can be wrought into a great variety of work, and is suitable for boxes, paper-knives, crosses, marquetry, baskets, book-covers, etc., and cuts clean and easily. A natural oil in this wood causes it to hold glue very poorly, yet in a dry place it does not warp or split to any extent, and it can be highly polished. Satinwood forms a handsome contrast with ebony, tulip, rosewood and some others of decided color.

TULIP-WOOD.

Tulip-wood, not our North American wood, but a variety from Brazil, is well adapted for fine effect. It has about the same gummy fibre as rosewood; the color is reddish, striped with darker shades very much like the tulip flower. A pleasant fancy is to inlay this wood with holly, ebony or similar woods, as representations of Autumn leaves, and, in fact, it is a very suitable wood for marquetry of almost all devices, but the handsome tints are apt to fade.

COCABOLA.

Cocabola is about as hard as tulip wood, but more resinous, and the sawdust will stain like a dye. It is of a dull red color, though slightly striped, and can be used like tulip wood for inlaying Autumn leaves, and it has the advantage of being considerably less in cost, and will take a handsome polish. It is quite apt to warp, and, like almost all the highly colored woods, will fade when long exposed to strong light.

OLIVE-WOOD.

Olive-wood, with its rich wavy tints, giving it the appearance of variegated marble, is an expensive material, much like box in texture. It is oily and unctuous, easily cut, and quite suitable for trinkets, paper-knives, jewelry and small articles, but being frequently unsound is more costly in large pieces. Some which is claimed to be brought from the Holy Land brings as much as three dollars per square foot. Large quantities of bijouterie, desks, fans, crosses, made of this wood, were sold at the Centennial Exhibition, much of which might have been vastly improved by tasty fret-saw treatment. For marquetry and carved work, olive-wood is a splendid material, and the skillful fret-sawyer can work out beautiful designs of Bible, prayer-book and hymn-book covers, which being made of this wood will serve to carry out the sentiment which we must all feel, that in the eternal fitness of things no other wood can take the place of that from the tree under the shade of which He who is the inspiration of all, sought retirement on the Mount of Olives.

BIRD'S-EYE MAPLE.

Bird's-eye Maple is a close grained gritty wood, capable of high polish, but requiring much labor and filling. It is difficult to work with a hand-saw, and requires careful skill even with a treadle machine, as the small knots drag upon the saw, causing it to run unevenly. The most satisfactory way to use it is veneered upon some other wood, otherwise it is very apt to warp and twist.

HUNGARIAN ASH.

Hungarian Ash is one of those splendid woods now much in vogue, and for groundwork in marquetry it is eminently suitable. As the figure greatly varies in some of this wood, the price of the more beautiful specimens is double that of ordinary grades. The grain is not very close, but disposed in waved lines, soft in some spots and hard in others. It is a difficult wood to cut, and is better adapted for backgrounds than for sawing. The most convenient way of using it is veneered on other woods, just as we have suggested for bird's-eye maple.

AMBOYNA.

Amboyna, which must complete our description of woods, and otherwise called *Kaibooca* wood, is imported from Singapore, and appears to be the excrescence or burr of some large tree. It is sawn in slabs from three inches square to twelve by twenty inches, is tolerably hard, and full of small curls and knots. The color varies from orange to chestnut brown, and sometimes reddish brown, and it is a highly ornamental wood, much prized in China and India for the construction of boxes, writing-desks and other ornamental work, in the same manner as we use it. As it is costly, we will also suggest that this wood be used as a veneer.

There are many other useful and ornamental woods easily to be procured from the dealers, which we cannot spare space to describe.

We will, however, suggest to the reader to collect, as far as possible, select specimens of the various sorts, small oblong pieces, which being duly labeled with the common and botanical names and some descriptive remarks that are pertinent to each, will afford an excellent means of instruction and amusement.

IVORY.

There are other materials which the fret-sawyer will find convenient and useful for sundry purposes, as ivory and tortoise-shell. Of *Elephant Ivory* there are two varieties, Asiatic and African, the latter being of a more opaque, dead white appearance than the other. The hippopotamus supplies ivory which is much harder and far more valuable than that of the elephant, being of a purer white, and almost free from grain. Ivory requires seasoning similar to that of wood, and is very liable to crack and warp when subjected to changes of temperature. It is useful for marquetry, but the value increases greatly with the size. It can be obtained of the dealers, cut to order, at about six or eight dollars per pound, the weight being taken in the rough state.

TORTOISE-SHELL.

Tortoise-shell is applicable to the same purposes as ivory. It is a substance supplied by the hawk-bill turtle, and differs in color. The animal itself is usually about a yard long and three-quarters wide. The shell consists of thirteen principal plates, composed of one or more layers, making the ordinary thickness about a quarter of an inch. It is quite brittle, as is also ivory, and must be tempered before working, by steeping it in boiling water for a few minutes, a process not at all allowable with ivory, which would thereby be spoiled and cracked.

MOTHER-OF-PEARL.

Mother-of-pearl is another of these choice materials. The layers of this substance can be split apart, but the pieces thus obtained, following the curvature of the shell, must be reduced to a smooth surface upon a wet grindstone. It is a beautiful material for inlaying, and may be wrought into delicate jewelry, etc.

Brass, gold and silver can also be used by the fret-sawyer, many beautiful ornaments being produced from these materials.

The reader will notice that we state no prices for the woods enumerated. There are regular reliable dealers who furnish these materials ready planed to any requisite thickness, and who will upon application also supply price lists, from which a selection can be made. They may be found among advertisers generally.

The woods most commonly used by the amateur are white holly and black walnut, which constitute the stock in trade of more than five-sixths of the fret-sawyers of the country, and the thicknesses mostly selected by them vary from an eighth to half an inch, more especially the former, as two or more pieces may be cut at one time with a great saving of labor.

RUBBER.

Hard vulcanized India-rubber is now manufactured in sheets about two feet square, and is applicable also for many purposes of fret-work. Toughness of fibre is not its least advantage, and it can be easily cut with small risk of breaking, because it has no definite grain, while a capability of fine polish renders it very attractive and convenient to use for jewelry, card-baskets, etc.; we have even known of a handsome clock-case made of this material. The texture being very fine and close, considerable friction is produced by sawing it, and, therefore, it will be a double advantage to oil the saw-blade frequently, to reduce the friction, and at the same time give somewhat of a polish to the inside edges, which might be impracticable after the design is cut out. These sheets of hard rubber are finely polished on the surface, but the track of the saw-blade is marked by a dull rusty-brown hue. The oil used upon the saw-blade will change this brown to black, just as walnut is rendered darker by the application of oil. The surplus oil will be absorbed by the rubber quite as freely as if applied in the more usual way with a bit of cloth.

Hard rubber is sold by the pound, and is measured by guage or decimals of the inch, thus: .10, .20, .30, .40, .60 guage signifies 1-10, 1-20, etc., of an inch in thickness. A square foot of 30-guage will weigh about seven or eight ounces.

DESIGN FOR A CROSS.

CHAPTER II.

Of Saws, Saw-Frames and Treadle Machines.

None will deny that a skillful workman must have a complete acquaintance with his tools and their capabilities. He will receive long lists of testimonials setting forth the manifold merits of variously constructed implements, but his knowledge of mechanical laws will be the safest guide and the best of all recommendations. He will not be vain in his own conceit, but, understanding how long a ladder that of improvement is, carefully examine cause and effect, and seek a reason for every screw or crank or wheel, and comprehend whether any part is too long or too short, too thick or too thin. It is such knowledge, won at the school of experience, that produces skill in anything.

First, let us consider the *saw-blades*, comprising about fifteen sizes, the first eight or nine of which are used in ordinary fret-sawing. They are of German and Swiss manufacture, and are so variable that, whenever they can be procured of good quality, it will always be more satisfactory and cheaper to purchase at least half a gross at once, *if they are fully up to standard*. First-rate saw-blades can be obtained at one dollar to one dollar and a quarter per gross, at wholesale, and poorer qualities, at half the price, are worth nothing. They should be sharp and true, fairly tempered, of good *blue* steel, and elastic. If too highly tempered, like some people possessing the same quality, they will snap and fly about in the most unpleasant manner. Good hoop-skirt wire has about the right temper. Some saws in a bunch will be cut better than others, and a good plan is to assort them. With a little practice, by passing the **toothed** edge over your thumb-nail, you will quickly learn the difference. Divide the stock of fret-saws, of each number, into two or three grades, and it will be found a saving of time, work and patience. First, cut them all of the proper length, and fold each grade in a paper by itself, just as needles are packed, and let each be appropriately marked with the number and grade. *A* will comprise such as are admirably sharp, suitable for soft woods, walnut, mahogany, etc. *B* will indicate those which are less sharp, and may be used for ivory, bone, metal or exceedingly hard, gritty woods, in the cutting of which, hardly the best saw will hold a sharp tooth. If there be any left from the selections *A* and *B*, mark them *C*, and use for hacking purposes. It is seldom, indeed, that all of one package will run alike, and the workman will find it extremely awkward to frequently change his saw while in use. A smooth, clear cut produces nice work, and it is obvious to any one that fret-sawing is not blacksmithing.

Upon the proper *tension* of the saw-blade depends its action. For this purpose a number of frames, in various styles, have been invented. Some of these are exceedingly simple in construction, some are combined with machinery and operated by foot-power, some are fine, some are rather clumsy, and it is from the entire assortment, we propose that the artizan may select such as may prove best adapted to the projected work. If a machine or implement violates any of the inexorable laws of mechanics, it will only give vexation of spirit and waste of labor.

HOME-MADE HAND FRAMES.

Here is an illustration of a hand-frame, which can be *home-made* at small cost. It is not monopolized by any patentee, and any one who is at all clever at the use of carpenter tools can make one according to the description:

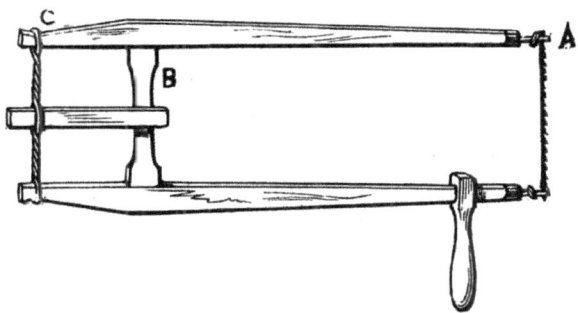

Procure two strips of well-seasoned, straight-grained maple, each about two feet long and fully one inch wide and thick. Plane them tapering and perfectly true, so they shall each be one-half an inch square at the end where the saw-blade is to be fastened. At the point where the brace B is joined to the two arms, the full dimensions of the wood (one inch) should be allowed, as the greatest strain will be there. From B to the tail of the frame, each arm should again taper to a half inch. Neatly round off the edges, leaving the under side of each arm flat for a couple of inches at B, so that the brace may be closely fitted.

Now we must connect the two arms with the brace; therefore, take a bit of maple nine inches long and one inch square, work it straight and true to this shape,

cutting a perfectly true, flat tenon one inch long and three-eighths of an inch thick at each end, as shown in the illustration, and hollowing or chamfering the edges of the brace, for the sake of neatness. About five inches from the tail end of each arm, cut a neat and perfectly true mortise for the tenons of the brace, and fit it in tightly, with glue and wooden or iron pegs, being careful that the tips of the arms are exactly perpendicular, otherwise the saw will cut crookedly.

Now, if we fasten a saw-blade to this frame at A, the leverage will be too great upon B, without a compensating balance at the other end, very much on the principle of a see-saw plank, which requires a boy at each end. This is one of the most simple yet important axioms of natural philosophy, and is applicable in more ways than we can count. The most inexpensive way to achieve this balance for our saw-frame, is by means of a twisted cord. Get a piece of stout cord (catgut would be better), tie the two ends together strongly, making it into a loop just large enough to go over the ends of the frame at C about a quarter inch. Whittle a stout flat bit of wood, six inches long, a quarter inch thick, and one inch wide; place it between the two strands of the cord, and begin to twist it around, enough to make it just taut, and let the stick, which, in mechanical nomenclature, is called *a key*, protrude far enough to rest against the brace and prevent the cord from untwisting. There will be only a slight strain upon the arms. A neat handle should now be made of this shape:

Take a bit of hard, tough wood, about one and a quarter inches square, six inches long; at one end bore a straight hole, a trifle larger than half an inch in diameter. Work down the remainder of the wood to form a neat handle, as in the illustration. Pass one arm of the frame through the hole, and, when it fits snugly, fasten the handle with a small screw, taking care that it is exactly perpendicular and hangs straight downwards. If a very neat job is desirable, which will add to the strength, let the end of the handle through which the hole is bored be made round, and narrow metal bands or ferrules driven on, one each side of the hole, rendering the wood less liable to split.

The next step will be to provide some appliance, as a clamp, to hold the saws. A very good article of this sort can be obtained from the hardware stores in large cities, at about twenty-five or thirty cents per pair. A cut of one is given here:

They have shanks about two inches long, part of which is cut with a screw-thread, and a small thumb-nut and screw furnishes the gripe. Having procured a pair of clamps, drill a straight hole lengthwise in the end of each arm at A, exactly in the centre, and having fitted on each arm a small brass or iron ferrule, to prevent the wood from splitting, screw in the clamps firmly, slightly oiling them, that they may move more easily inward. Smooth off all rough places with sand-paper, and, if you have followed the directions carefully, you will have a very satisfactory saw-frame and a valuable lesson in practical mechanics, costing less than half a dollar.

Those whose skill and ingenuity do not reach even this small extent, can purchase a frame from the hardware shops, at various prices, and made of wood or steel, ranging from a dollar upwards. They are not toys, but good, serviceable tools, capable of any work within their scope. The arms should be free from all flaws, not too elastic, and there ought to be plenty of sweep from the blade to the back of the frame, *at least* 14 inches. Swiss or piercing saw-frames are not convenient for fret-sawing, as they have only about two or three inches sweep.

SWISS FRAME.

The steel frames are imported, and one of twenty inches sweep, will cost three or four dollars. They possess the merits of being very durable, not at all liable to spring or warp, and, as will be seen by the following illustration, one of the clamps is movable, so that it can be lowered to suit a short saw blade:

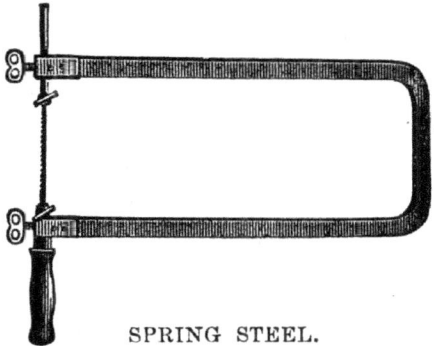

SPRING STEEL.

The wooden frames do not vary much from the description already given. A figure of one is here shown, which is the cheapest made, and sells for one dollar.

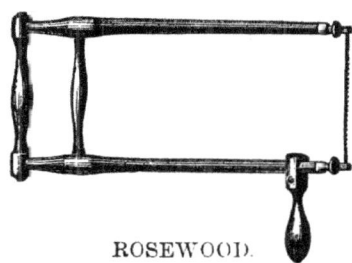

ROSEWOOD.

They are quite as serviceable as any other hand-frame.

To any one whose purse may be adequate to his ambition, the treadle or foot-power machines offer great temptations. The principles that govern their structure, are almost identical with those of the hand-frame. They are not all perfect, and the increasing demand may yet call forth one that shall be the acme of all that is desirable. We know of fret-sawyers who have builded their own treadle-machines, in preference to buying any of those sold.

We have a boughten one, and are now building one with improvements which we feel are needed.

Now, let us consider some of the characteristics of the treadle-machines. First, they should not be a pound heavier than necessary; they should run perfectly easy and true, with the least possible vibration, for oftentimes the width of fretwork will require to be no wider than a line, or, one-twelfth of an inch, so that a single false cut with the saw, will ruin the work entirely. The tension should be reciprocal, and with the same strain both up and down. Those who have seen two men working with an old-fashioned pit-saw, may have noticed that the man outside the pit pulls just at the same time the sawyer below pushes the saw upward, and so they go, up and down, regular as the beat of a pendulum, each doing his fair share of the labor. Any disagreement in their efforts would waste their strength, while perfect unity of movement renders the task easy. The same principle is quite applicable to the fret-saw-machine, and, in some of those manufactured, it is accomplished by means of steel springs; in others, the elasticity of iron is depended upon, for the same effect, though, in our own humble opinion, when the arms are movable, hard wood is preferable to iron, except that the *bearings*, the fulcrums upon which the two levers work, should be of hard metal, lest they wear away too fast.

The simple arrangement of a crank guides the saw-frame up and down; or movable spindles, carrying the saw firmly clamped, are fitted to sockets which are parts of a stationary frame, and, in the latter case, tension is acquired by the aid of strong steel springs, as before mentioned. The superiority of these treadle-machines is due to a degree of steadiness and mathematical exactness which can only be acquired by long practice with a hand-frame. Both hands can be used to guide the work, which is a positive advantage, and the speed is much greater. Some of them are so compact that the whole apparatus does not weigh more than ten or twelve pounds, and can be conveniently carried about in a small package, while others are unnecessarily heavy, with a needless weight of iron work. We bought one of the best, long ago, and though we have detected faults which our fastidious mind deplored, yet has it been a faithful servitor nearly four years, almost in daily use, and is now perfectly sound and good. When we say *best*, we mean an evidence of strict regard for true mechanical laws, which vary not, whatever they may be applied to. Studious men have found them out, and they have become the servants of mankind, for happiness, behoof or benefit.

As usual, these machines are patented, though the prices generally are not exorbitant. Yet there are many clever people who may be zealous to utilize their own tact and ingenuity; therefore, we will offer some suggestions to help them.

A HOME-MADE TREADLE MACHINE.

Procure two pieces of maple, just as we described for the hand-frame. Work them up in the same way for a pair of arms. Now we shall have some work for the iron-founder, in a few castings requisite. From a bit of pine board whittle out a pattern in this shape,

about eight inches long, two inches at the widest part, and half an inch thick. Fit to it, three inches from one end, at right angles and perfectly square, a piece of this shape, fastening it with brads,

making the entire pattern, as seen by a side view, thus:

PATTERN NO. 1.

Now, make another pattern, of this shape,

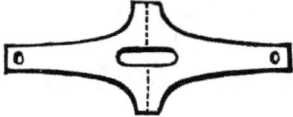

five inches long, five-sixteenths thick, three-quarters wide at the ends, and two inches across the centre. Where the dotted line is seen, you will fasten on a small V-shaped ridge, one-quarter by three-eighths of an inch, thus:

PATTERN NO. 2.

With these patterns, which must be square and true, have two iron castings made of No. 2 and one of No. 1. They will cost about eight or ten cents per pound. It would be well to mark a light groove across each end of No. 1, perfectly straight, as it will serve as a guide in filing up the centre. The castings will be given to you rough, and you must finish them off with a file.

With a triangular file trim up the grooves across the ends of No. 1, observing to keep them perfectly true, often testing the cut, with a try-square. Then also file the ridges of No. 2, to make the best possible fit to the grooves of No. 1, thus:

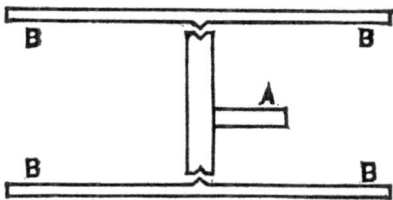

In the step A, three holes must be drilled, for by it the castings will be held to the table with screws. Similar holes must be bored also at B, of the parts No. 2, by which they can be fastened to the inside of the arms, and it would be well to have these holes at B rather oval than round, so that the arms may be more truly adjusted, as the heads of the screws that fasten the castings to the arms, will hold firmly enough. All the holes should be countersunk or beveled. Having fitted and fastened the castings, procure, if possible, a second-hand sewing-machine-table, with drive-wheel and treadle. They can frequently be purchased at junk-shops for a dollar each. Then neatly screw the casting first mentioned, No. 1, by means of the step A, firmly to the back of the table, at about the centre. The arms should then be attached in the following manner: Procure two pieces of stout wire, ten and a half inches long and about three-sixteenths thick, and, if you cannot do it yourself, get a locksmith to cut a screw-thread on one end of each piece for about one inch and a half; have a small thumb-nut fitted to each screw-end, and rivet a small iron washer to the opposite ends. Now, cut two holes in each of the arms as large as the thickness of the wire, of somewhat conical shape, and pass the wire through them, with the screw-ends at the top, fastening them with thumb-nuts. The structure will then present this appearance:

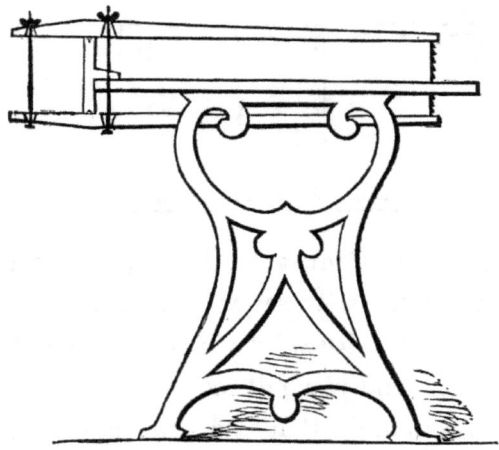

The conical holes are so shaped to give free play to the tension-rods. All that now remains is a small wooden platform of this shape,

which should be screwed to the front of the table, so that the saw-blade, when clamped (which can be done by the same means described for the hand-frame), will freely move through a small hole in the exact centre of the platform. And you will also have a couple of castings made of the following shape:

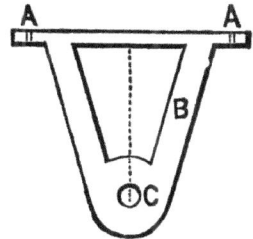

Technically, such a fixture is called a *hanger*. It should be half an inch thick, measure six inches in the direction of the dotted line and about four inches from A to A, at which points, holes should be drilled for screws to fasten each of these hangers to the under side of the table. At C, a hole must be drilled very true, for they are to serve as bearings for a small shaft, about half an inch in diameter. At one end of the shaft is to be fitted a small pulley, and at the other end an eccentric of about two inches diameter, one inch from the center of which is fastened a short flat bit of hard wood, by means of a set-screw through one end, while the other end is fastened to the lower arm of the saw-frame by a screw, upon which the short connecting strip will move rather loosely. Attach a round leather belt to the driving-wheel and the small pulley, and the gearing will then be as shown on next page.

The machine, having been carefully oiled, is now ready for work. When fitting the connecting piece to the lower arm, the proper length may be determined by moving the saw-frame down, so that the end of the upper arm shall be within three-quarters of an inch from the table, and the set-screw in the eccentric shall be downward. Cut the connecting piece just long enough to measure

between the lower arm and the set-screw of the eccentric, allowing room so that the lower arm may not strike against the under side of the table.

Though the manufacture of such a machine may be easy for any one who is clever with the use of ordinary tools, yet we would recommend, if possible, the purchase of one of those made by skillful workmen, and with an exactness that machinery only will give. We offer the description, however, and a calculation of the probable cost:

Two hard-wood arms	15
Castings, about 5 pounds	40
Tension-rods and nuts (can be bought in any city)	30
Pulley and eccentric, say	75
Sewing-machine-table, about	$1 00
Steel rod for shaft	10
Screws, clamps, etc., etc.	1 00
	$3 70

Experiments are costly; therefore, we earnestly advise a "boughten machine," when within the capacity of one's purse. Some of the treadle-machines have not sufficient sweep, so that work which is an inch or two longer than usual cannot readily pass the brace or tail of the frame. To obviate this, turn the saw-blade around, so that the cutting edge is in the opposite direction, and so work the other way; otherwise the teeth of the saw-blade should be facing the operator.

DESIGN FOR WALL POCKET.

CHAPTER III.

OTHER TOOLS AND IMPLEMENTS.

The principal outlay will be for a good hand-saw or treadle-machine, all the other tools being quite inexpensive. A fine awl, 10 cents, or a far better tool at $1.00, called the Archimedean drill-stock, with four or five drills of different sizes,

and is useful in many ways; three or four files, round, half-round, square and triangular, fine cut and about three inches long; the cutting-board, with a malleable iron clamp attached, to fasten it to a table or some firm support. The cutting-board is a piece of walnut or hard wood half-inch thick board, about ten inches wide and eighteen inches long, of the following shape:

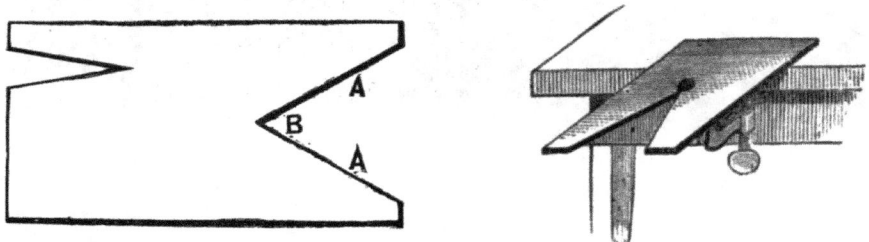

The V-shaped opening is needed, so that the saw can be kept working at B, and easily sawing to the right or left, while the work finds a support at A, A and B, and is saved from breakage. These extras will be required, when a hand-saw frame is used. The best treadle-machines are now provided with boring attachments of various merits, which are run by the same power as the saw, and also have tables which are perfectly true, so that with ordinary care, the cut of the saw is perfectly straight through the work, which is not accomplished by hand without considerable practice. Files are not requisite for treadle-machines, as the work is much more exactly and cleanly cut. We venture to suggest that neat, careful hand-work needs no filing, except when further wrought by carving, of which we shall speak anon.

Our love for home-made conveniences prompts the mention of one handy thing to tax the ingenuity of the artizan. It is a contrivance which our own need invented, as a sort of screw-press, in which glued work can be adjusted and left to dry, while many other uses, to which it may be adapted, will make this simple apparatus worth far more than it costs.

Get four strips of well-seasoned hard wood, one inch wide, fully half an inch thick, and about twenty inches long. In each piece, about one and a half inches from *each* end, cut a recess one inch long and half an inch deep, into which fit a strip of hard wood, about four or five inches long, forming two frames like the following:

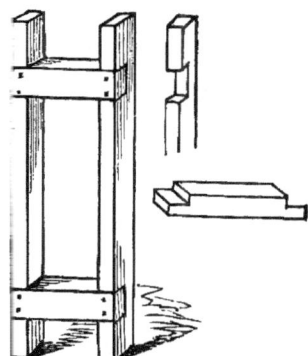

Procure two strips of hard wood, two feet or more long, at least one inch thick, and exactly as wide as the space between the strips that form the uprights. At any hardware store you can purchase a joiner's wooden clamp for about thirty cents. This will furnish the screw and nut, which latter will be merely one of the jaws of the clamp. Bore a hole through one of the long strips, exactly in the centre, a trifle larger than the diameter of the screw, and fasten the jaw of the clamp directly under it. Then, by slipping the frames over the ends of the long strips, the press will stand as follows:

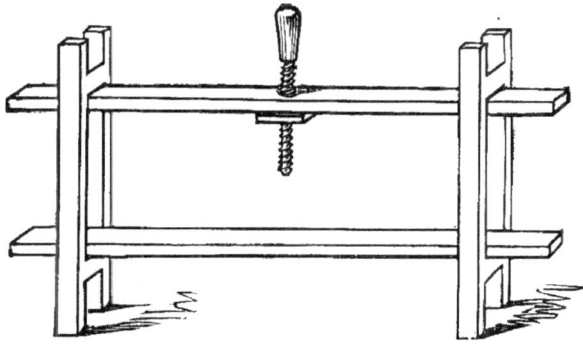

A few square wooden blocks and a couple of square pieces of

plank will be found convenient to use with it. You will readily see that, various parts being movable, this press is adapted for large or small articles which are to be glued. A six-inch strip, fastened transversely at the bottom of each standard, will serve as a foot to keep it upright and steady. Of course, the proportions stated can be varied to suit the taste.

The effect of fret-work is often rendered more beautiful by careful and judicious touches of carving-tools, of which we will give a brief description. Those manufactured in England by S. J. Addis are the best. They can be purchased in this country either singly or in sets suitable for general work, comprising eighteen tools, at about six dollars. The accompanying illustration will show the different shapes, and we may further describe the use of some of them by the numbers:

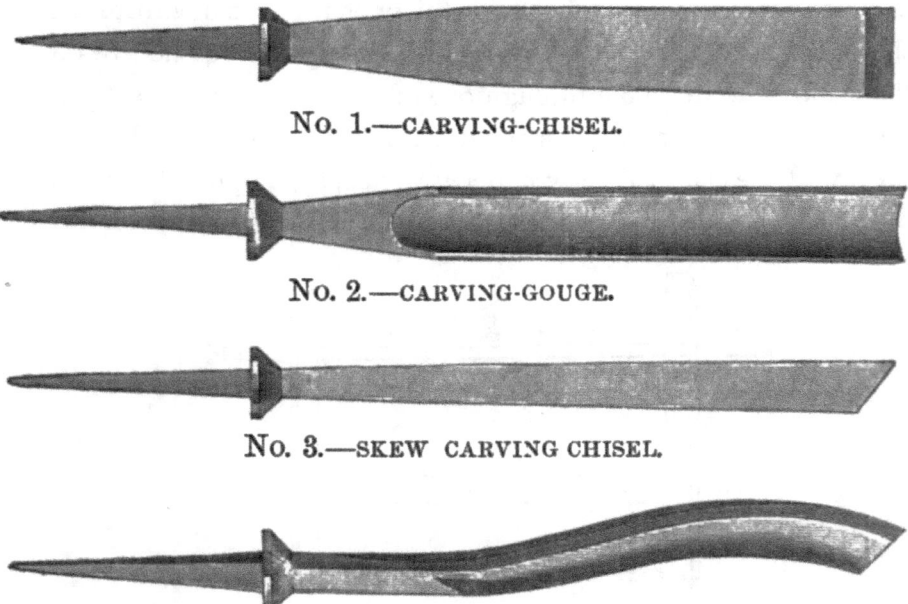

No. 1.—CARVING-CHISEL.

No. 2.—CARVING-GOUGE.

No. 3.—SKEW CARVING CHISEL.

No. 4—BENT PARTING-TOOL.

FRET-SAWING FOR PLEASURE AND PROFIT. 41

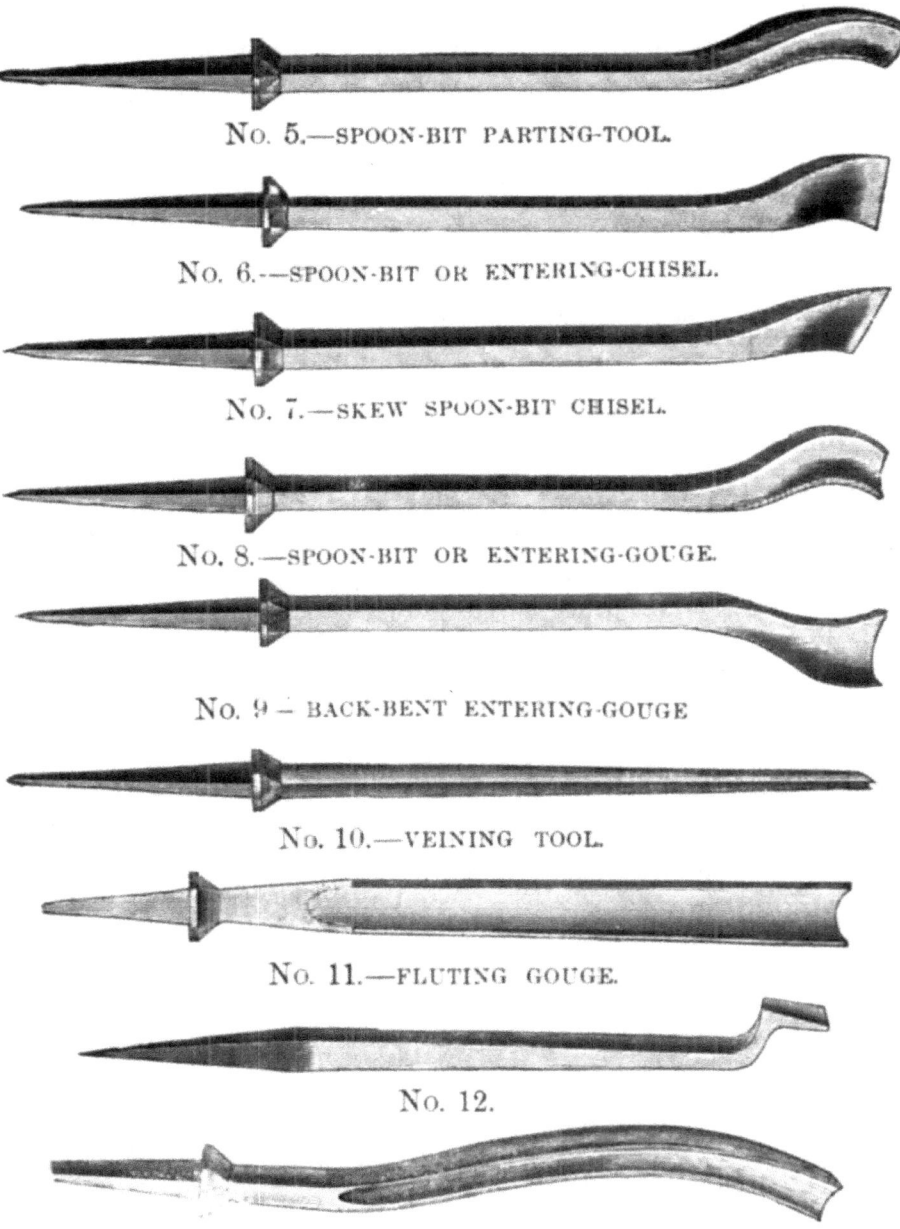

No. 5.—SPOON-BIT PARTING-TOOL.

No. 6.—SPOON-BIT OR ENTERING-CHISEL.

No. 7.—SKEW SPOON-BIT CHISEL.

No. 8.—SPOON-BIT OR ENTERING-GOUGE.

No. 9.—BACK-BENT ENTERING-GOUGE.

No. 10.—VEINING TOOL.

No. 11.—FLUTING GOUGE.

No. 12.

No. 13.—DOUBLE BENT FLUTING GOUGE.

No. 1.—The chisel is of various widths, from one-eighth to an inch, has a straight edge, and is used for plane surfaces which are square, removing superfluous wood and grounding. It is the most necessary tool of the set.

No. 2—The gouge has a curved edge of various sweeps, according to the depth to be cut. It ranges from almost flat to the exact half a circle, about eight different sweeps.

No. 3—The skew-chisel is a variation of No. 1, the edge being ground back from either corner, being right or left hand. It is useful for working out the inside corners of angles, where the edge of No. 1 would be too wide.

No. 4.—The parting-tool is a sort of gouge with an angular edge. Its cut is V-shaped, and it is quite essential for various purposes of cutting angular grooves. They are made either straight or bent. No. 10 is only a variation of the parting-tool, quite narrow, and used to engrave the veins of leaves and similar work. The parting-tool is often used for the same purpose.

Nos. 6, 7, 8, 9, 12, 13 are simple variations of those tools already mentioned. Their peculiar shape adapts them for use in confined spaces, where the shanks of the other tools could not be carried back far enough to make a clear cut, the relief of the carving being in the way.

There is a tool, used by wood-engravers. called the mezzotinto-scraper, which will be found very convenient. Its name explains its use, and we shall speak of it anon.

MEZZOTINTO SCRAPER.

There are nooks and corners where sand-paper cannot be used, and for such work a riffler is requisite:

As the engraving shows, it is simply a file with a variation like the cutting-tools 6, 7, 8, etc. They cost forty or fifty cents each.

Bracket Design in Leaf Work and Wood Carving.

CHAPTER IV.

OIL-STONES, ETC.

The sharpening of tools will require oil-stones, of which the Arkansas stone is the best, as it is very hard and fine-grained. If you examine such a stone under a microscope, you can see these grains, which will appear like sand-paper. Each of these infinitesimal grains presents a cutting edge harder than the tools themselves, so that the constant attrition wears away the steel, and the tool becomes what we call *sharp*. Further examination with the microscope, will show that the edge has become full of serratures or teeth, from the minute grooves cut by the sharp grains of the stone. If these grains are coarse, the grooves will be coarse also, as will naturally be understood. In obedience to this principle, oil-stones should be kept clean and protected from any dirt or grit that may find its way to the surface and show its presence by certain irregular grooves upon the edge of the metal, which greatly vex our patience.

Select a good oblong Arkansas stone, free from flaws; make a neat covered box for it, and wipe it clean every time you finish using it. They are made of various shapes, and it will be necessary to procure one with a round edge, like the illustration, for sharpening the inside of gouges:

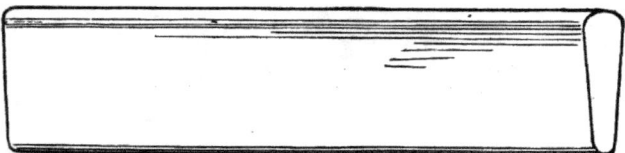

Where expense is an objection, this stone, having a flat side, may be used instead of the one first mentioned.

A pencil point will also be essential. They are short pieces, about a quarter-inch square, with one end worked down to a sharp, round point, and are very convenient for edges which are angular or of insufficient compass for the action of larger stones. Chisels should be ground to a true bevel, at about an angle of 20 degrees. Put a few drops of clean sweet-oil upon the stone, and then, holding the bevel of the tool flat upon it, with a little pressure of the hand move the tool forward and backward, taking care to avoid tilting the handle up or down, and not bearing more on one side than on the other, lest in either case you work away the bevel. Gouges are sharpened in a similar way, but, the edge being round, a rocking motion is given to the tool, to prevent the formation of a number of angular points upon the edge.

Occasionally the steel of which the tool is made, being somewhat softer than desirable, a tiny wire edge will appear upon the flat edge. Now there is grit also in leather, and a few strokes upon a smooth strip of calf-skin will remove this wire edge, in the same way as razors are sharpened with a strap. The forming of any bevel upon this edge must be avoided, for we know of but one case where double bevels are useful, and that is in turning-chisels.

For some carving work, a small mallet may at times be convenient, and a suitable one can be made of a smooth square block of box, lignum-vitæ, or other hard wood. It need not be more than two inches square at each end, and about two and a half inches long. Bore a hole for a neatly whittled handle, and fit it tight.

Design for Cross in White Holly or Colored Velvet.

CHAPTER V.

Of Glue, Polish, Sand-Paper, Paste, Etc.

It is not our purpose to oppose or to be wise above what is written, but our own actual experience, as well as that of dealers in the article, sustain us in denying that *white* glue is the strongest. The very dark Cologne glue possesses the greatest strength of all, and in every case, where the color dark brown is allowable, it is preferable to any other. Glue is rendered white by a bleaching process, which decreases its strength, and it is used for such manufactures as require a mere size, and in which strength is of little moment. The easiest and best way to melt glue is to break it into pieces sufficiently small, put them into an earthenware vessel, just cover them with warm water, and set them aside until the glue is thoroughly soaked and forms a stiff jelly. Then pour off all the surplus water, put the jelly into a double glue-pot, and place it on the stove to melt. The outside receptacle of the glue-pot must be filled with hot water, for it is very easy to spoil the glue by roasting or cooking. It should only be melted at a temperature not higher than boiling water, and not in any excess of supply at one time, as frequent melting diminishes its strength. When applied to any work, it should be quite hot, and of such a consistency that it will just hardly drop from the brush. The pieces to be joined should be warmed, so that the glue will not chill suddenly, and only a thin coat of it applied. If the shape of the work will allow, it must then be immediately fastened in the press already described, confined with clamps or tied with strings, and left until the glue is perfectly dry. Wherever the thickness of the wood will allow it, small holes should be drilled, not quite through the wood, and wooden pegs of the same color driven in carefully, which will afford an additional hold.

Polishing is easy work after a little practice and attentive notice of the effect. French polish is made in the following mode:

Two oz. picked shellac, 1 oz. gum-arabic, $\frac{1}{2}$ oz. gum-copal, $1\frac{1}{2}$ pints spirits of wine.

Dissolve the gums thoroughly in the spirits, and strain all through a bit of fine muslin. It should not be quite as thick as molasses, and can be thinned with more spirits. This will give a light-colored polish if the gums are pure and good.

If a darker color is desired, substitute one ounce gum-benzoin for the gum-arabic and copal, and use only one pint of spirits If it is required to further color the polishes, it may be done by the addition of dragon's-blood.

French polishing is done with a rubber, consisting of a few folds of cloth, being moistened with the polish, and a thin linen rag placed over it, on which are poured a few drops of raw linseed-oil, and the whole is applied evenly on the surface of the work with a circular motion. This polish dries quickly, and, when dried out, more of it must be applied to the rubber, as before. Porous wood will take up a great deal of it, and, if economy is any object, a very thin previous coat of sizing will fill the pores. Two or more applications of the polish, thinly applied, will show more finely than one thick coat. All work which is to be oiled, polished or varnished, must be first rubbed as smooth as possible with very fine sand-paper; otherwise every little imperfection of the grain in the wood will exhibit itself to critical eyes. When the work is too delicate to bear any strain or pressure, it is best to partly polish the wood before cutting out the design, and give it a finish subsequently, though in nine cases out of ten, a skillful hand will do all the polishing afterward, and without damage to the work. The polished surface must present an even appearance, as nothing looks so unworkmanlike as blotches and streaks, and when there are any such they must be well rubbed down with an oiled cloth. Only enough oil is needed throughout the whole operation to cause the rubber to glide along easily without adhering to the surface, which would produce unsightly daubs.

The artizan will find it expedient to use judgment in the finish of his work, and not use polish, oil or varnish indiscriminately. Some work shows better with the plain wood, while a true idea of Art would dictate further manipulation, only when some more beautiful effect can be reached, exhibiting more clearly the grain or the color of the material. Raw linseed-oil may frequently be used to good purpose. It should be applied in limited quantity, so that the surface shall not present a greasy appearance. The pores of the wood having become filled, scarcely any further application is necessary. A mere shiny appearance should be strictly shunned in every case. French polishing cannot be well performed with a brush, as the process depends altogether upon patient and continued rubbing.

Sand-paper is too well known to describe. The finest, 00, is almost smooth, and thence it is graded by half-numbers up to 3, which is very coarse. It should be carefully applied, with only a light pressure, lest it wear away the surface unequally. A convenient holder for sand-paper can be made with two oblong pieces of hard wood, three-eighths thick, and of any convenient size. In the one intended for the bottom, fix an inch and a half wood screw exactly in the middle, sinking the head a little below the surface. At each end of the other piece fasten three small steel pins, with points filed sharp, and let them protrude about three-sixteenths; bore a hole in the centre, the size of the screw. Place the top piece over the lower one, fitting a small wooden knob to the screw, which will serve to keep the two pieces from coming asunder while in use, and also for a handle to hold it by. A piece of sand-paper can be placed upon the bottom, just long enough to lap over and be held by the sharp points. The bottom piece should be somewhat curved toward each end, so that a sharp edge may not injure any part of the work.

Common wheat flour paste is all that can be desired for applying designs. It should be somewhat thick, and made in small quantities, as it soon turns sour. Mucilage is not at all convenient or appropriate. A large tablespoonful of flour and half a pint of boiling water will make a large cupful of paste.

CHAPTER VI.

Of Designs.

The artizan will find no difficulty in obtaining patterns or designs, of which so many have recently been published. It will be certainly more profitable to secure such as are finely executed, and, if not already bound in book-form, at least collected into convenient shape, for we shall offer a suggestion by which original or purchased designs may be saved.

Lay the design to be copied flat and smooth upon a table or a wide board; cover it neatly with a piece of thin tissue-paper, fastening it down with artist's tacks, which may be obtained at about thirty cents a dozen. Let it be free from wrinkles. Trace the pattern through with a No. 2 Faber's or other good lead-pencil. If desirable, a sheet of prepared carbon or impression-paper *placed between pieces of tissue-paper* may be also laid beneath the design, thereby producing two or more copies.

The tissue-paper tracing can be easily fixed upon the wood, if a little care and patience are exercised. Let the paste (made of wheat flour) be rather thicker than usual, and brush it over the entire *surface of the wood.* It is difficult to describe in print, just how thick the paste should be, but it can be just wet enough to barely moisten the paper. The paste must be applied to the wood only, as the least stroke of the brush upon the thin paper would entirely spoil it. The design being correctly drawn, apply one edge of the tissue-paper to the pasted surface, carefully sweeping it on with a gentle motion of the hand, avoiding all wrinkles. When drying, the paper will shrink a little, which will render it quite smooth. We have tried this plan hundreds of times, and find it easy and convenient, as the paper can be subsequently removed, with great facility, by dampening it with a moist sponge, and a few rubs with sand-paper entirely obliterates all traces of the paste. On no account, would we ever trace the design directly upon the wood, as the least deviation of a line would disfigure light woods, and on the dark ones, the impression could hardly be seen.

Familiarity with outlines will increase by practice, and the artizan will discover many tasteful combinations may be possible. Oftentimes, we have found great advantage from deftly changing the general contour of a design, where our humble idea of fitness suggested an alteration as desirable. The finest designs now published are frequently drawn in quarter or half-sections, the skill of the artizan being taxed to delineate the balance, which is a good rule in affording an opportunity for the exercise of brains and good taste. We consider fret-sawing quite as much a fine art as painting, sculpture, or any of the fields for the exhibition of talent or skill, and it is worthy of patient, honest effort. We were taught in boyhood's days *never to whittle without making something*, and, though a perfect labyrinth of fine lines has sometimes seemed impossible, yet each difficulty overcome has left us yet seeking the ultimate capability of the fret-saw. A book of ornaments, silhouettes and other devices, recently issued by the publisher of this volume, seemed to us a vast encouragement, and, though doubtful at first, we have discovered in almost every design a susceptibility of reproduction in fret-work, if the master-hand touches it cunningly. We need this ornament; it elevates and teaches, and all such emotions smooth the rough places of life, rendering a tribute to the light of home. If time thus spent is a loss, then have Angelo, Raphael and Albert Durer lived in vain.

Design in Marquetry and Inlaying.

CHAPTER VII.

OF MARQUETRY.

This French word signifies, in plain English, inlaid work, an art which will afford full scope for your ambition and skill. The subject has scarcely been discussed heretofore, though the art is not at all new, and we shall hope to say as much as can be said ere we leave the artizan to his own reflections. With this, as with all other efforts, patience, perseverance and practice bring perfection. Damiano spent nine years in accomplishing his master-piece, the choir in the church of Domenico, at Bologna, a work unsurpassed hitherto, and that bears for its proud legend, "Fra Damianos fecit."

Let us essay to describe the means of accomplishing such rare beauty that holds the eye to a strong allegiance, and perhaps we shall learn what the cunning hand can do for Art, while rendering tributary the abundant and varied resources of Nature.

Inlaying requires as perfect steadiness as can be acquired, and therefore, a treadle-machine is better adapted for the purpose than a hand-saw frame. We shall first describe the process by the former, not at all forgetting to minister to the needs of those who possess only the latter, so that none may lack a tribute to Art. The designs are without limit. Birds, fruit, flowers of every hue,

ornaments with lace-work tracery, and everything that has symmetry and beauty afford the examples. Early specimens of this work were executed in woods of natural colors, but in later days dyed woods were used, which had the disadvantage of fading by age. Some splendid specimens were, nevertheless, exhibited in the Paris Exposition, of which the woods were stained by a peculiar method, making the colors permanent, as the dye penetrated to a considerable depth of the wood, which was impregnated with a weak solution of chloride of soda, and one-fifth part of pyrolignite added, to prevent warping. Dyed material possesses one great advantage. Different kinds of woods will shrink unequally, at last producing a defective joint; therefore, where the

same effect can be gained, it is preferable to use the same kind of wood for the inlay, and stain the various portions as may be suitable. For this purpose the ordinary aniline dyes such as the druggists sell, or any similar coloring matter, may be used. Shading is produced by immersing the pieces in hot sand, but is too experimental a process to describe with accuracy. The artizan is not prohibited from trying it, and we will endeavor to give a hint or two of the way. Fill a shallow iron pan with dry sand, and heat it on the stove, till it is hot enough to brown a bit of paper held in contact with it. Carefully apply the portions of inlay requiring to be shaded, in the same manner to the hot sand. It is evident, that the longer the wood is thus treated, the deeper the stain will be, and the scorching will be graduated, according to the immediate or direct contact with the sand. The process requires careful attention, and as a deeper tint can be obtained by a darker shade of the coloring matter, applied with a small pencil-brush, we consider it easier of performance.

Veneers are especially adapted for marquetry, though with them the thinness prevents beveling, a practice that is exceedingly convenient, when the wood is thicker than one-sixteenth of an inch. Yet as we proceed it will be obvious that the work often dictates the thickness of material to be used. For the sake of illustration, let us take the simple design given here:

If you notice the letter, you will find that there are no lines that cross each other; therefore, it is called a *simple* design. When these lines do cross, so that there are one or more *cores*, the design is called *complex*, these *cores* being laid into the inlay.

The artizan having provided two pieces of sound wood, one light and one dark, will, if possible, have the one for the inlay slightly thicker than the other, or he may accomplish the intended effect, by pasting a piece of thick paper on the under side of the inlay piece. This precaution is only necessary for beveling. Now place the wood that is to form the G (see illustration) above that which is to serve for the ground, and, if the whole thickness is nearly a quarter-inch, fasten them together with tiny wire tacks, which may be obtained at the hardware stores for a few cents per ounce, and are only about as thick as a needle, being a quarter-inch long. Drive in a few, not quite through the wood, lest the points protrude from the under side. The only need of the tacks is to prevent the woods from slipping, and if the thickness is not sufficient the plan of glueing must be resorted to, as will be described for veneers. Of course a paper pattern of the design should be pasted to the top piece of wood.

The next step is to calculate the proper bevel, and in connection we give an illustration of an attachment to one of the treadle-machines:

BEVELING ATTACHMENT.

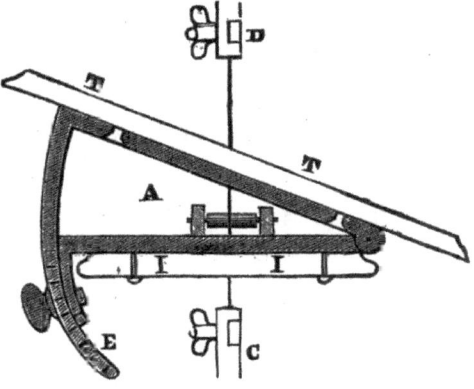

The principle is the same in all such attachments. Its use is to keep the table, T, at a certain angle, so that the inlay shall be somewhat wedge-shaped. To prove this angle, take two bits of waste wood, the same in thickness as that of the work intended, and saw out a small oval from them, doubled; if the angle is correct, the upper piece will drop into the lower one, fitting snugly. If it will not fit easily with a slight tap of a wooden mallet, the slope is too great; therefore the table must be lowered a trifle, and the trial made again, until the correct angle is determined, when the work can proceed. There is not the least difficulty in finding the angle, and it is far easier to accomplish, than for us to describe the process. At the point marked with a dotted line, bore a very small hole through the wood. With a little practice this can be done on a slant, so that when the work is finished no trace of the puncture will be seen:

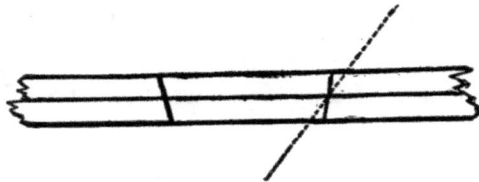

The dotted line of the figure represents the imperforation, which is only apparent in the waste pieces of the work. It requires a steady hand to do this, but it saves any unsightly plugging or filling the awl-hole, and the artizan should avail himself of every means to produce neat work.

Now start the saw (its cutting edge always facing you), and work around the design, preserving the slope of the bevel from *top* to *bottom*, and on no account going back with the saw, but continue cutting straight onward until the entire outline is cut through. The piece, sawed from the upper wood, will then measure the same at the bottom as the top of the piece from the ground, with the single exception of the space left by the track of the saw. To reduce this space, use (for double thickness of one eighth wood) a saw-blade not coarser than Nos. 1 or 2.

Now if it were not for the thick paper which we previously spoke of, we would need a greater bevel, which should be avoided, if possible, for if the inlay have too much flare, it will not be so apt to remain fixed in the ground. A few slight taps with a wooden mallet will suffice to drive it in tight, a *very slight* touch of glue being given to the edges. The work can then be scraped smooth with a cabinet-scraper, a small square plate of steel with

a sharp edge and rubbed well with fine sand-paper, further polishing being done, if desired or required by the character and style of the work. If care has been exercised, the line of junction, between the two woods, will be imperceptible to the naked eye.

Complex inlaying is done somewhat similar. As a very plain specimen, we give another letter, as shown above.

Here it will be perceived that there are lines crossing each other, forming an extra piece, A, called *a core*. Now it is evident that if the saw cuts this out, working in the same direction, as before mentioned, the under side of the inlay will be too wide and disproportionate; therefore, the simple way of avoiding it will be to cut exactly the opposite way, and fit the core in its place from the *under side*. The following diagram may plainly show this:

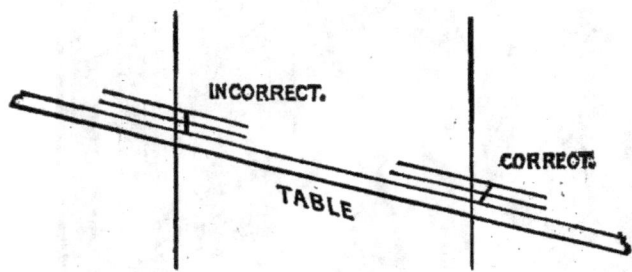

All the other directions are equally applicable as for simple inlaying, excepting that the perforation for entering the saw-blade will need to be filled with a tiny wooden plug, as *there will be no waste wood* around the core.

Perhaps it will be evident, from the preceding remarks, that such work requires more steadiness than can be reasonably expected, even after long practice, with the hand-saw frame. Those who may be zealous to try that otherwise extremely useful implement, can tilt their cutting-boards, so that the saw-blade, when held directly perpendicular, as it always should be, shall be at an acute instead of a right angle to the board, and if, even then, the bevel can be preserved exact and true, it will be a feat more difficult than imagined.

Veneers being scarcely thicker than one-thirty-second of an inch, will not admit of a beveled edge if used in single layers;

therefore, the table or board should be at a right angle to the saw-blade, of which as fine a one as possible should be used, so that the channel or kerf may be as narrow as possible. Several thicknesses may be cut at one time, and each of different wood, so that particular portions of the design can be afterward easily adjusted to the several parts of the ground. It will be more economical, if one kind of wood is used for the inlay, and each piece dyed its appropriate color and dried before it is set in the ground; otherwise the coloring matter might run from one piece to another, and blur the work. Care should be exercised, when staining

veneers, lest they warp, and a weight must be placed upon the moistened wood, until quite dry, and then each piece well fitted to its place. Dyed veneers, of various hues, can be procured from dealers in fine cabinet woods, but where waste is objectionable, it will be advantageous to stain each piece separately, after the entire pattern is cut out, in which case, one layer will serve as well as half a dozen.

Veneers are also glued to less expensive woods and sold by the dealers, or the artizan can prepare them himself, as we shall presently show. Their use is just the same as of any wood of equal thickness. When the colors are varied, for beveled work the least difficult mode is to repeat the process for each extra color, as advised for two thicknesses, if the tint is of the wood itself, but when merely stained, the operation is the same as with veneers.

If there are several pieces composing the design, it will be of advantage to match them together, if they are to join each other, before setting them finally into the ground, especially when veneers are used, and this for the simple reason of having the work all ready to put together. If the pieces are very small or delicate,

the greater part of the design can be formed by glueing them to a sheet of thin, stout paper, which will prevent delicate work from fracture, and preserve infinitesimal portions from being lost, as will often happen.

The process of veneering is very simple, but not too much so to do without attention. Let us suppose it is requisite to veneer a table-top with a wreath of flowers inlaid. The design having already been cut out, the staining and all other details finished, it is put together, as already directed, and a layer of thin but strong paper glued to the under side, and it must be perfectly smooth. The entire ground of the veneer should be a little larger than the table-top, to allow for waste. The next step is to get a smooth bit of plank, the same size as the top of the table. This is styled *a caul*, and cabinet-makers have them of various sizes and shapes; its purpose is to press the work, without indenting or bruising the veneer. Several clamps must also be provided, which consist of strong wooden bars, somewhat rounded on their inner edges, and connected by iron screw-bolts and nuts.

The surface of the table-top, and also the under surface of the veneer, are now scratched over with an iron toothing-plane, a queer instrument having an edge like a comb, which gives the surfaces some rough ridges, that serve to aid the glue in holding. Of course its use upon the papered veneer should be less than on bare wood.

The surface of the table-top being warmed and the veneer and caul made hot, the table-top is brushed over with thin glue, a coating of which is also applied to the veneer, which must be immediately placed on the table-top; upon the veneer is put the heated caul, and the clamping-bars applied and quickly screwed down, three or four inches apart. The heat of the caul keeps the glue in a fluid state, while the clamping-bars are being adjusted and screwed down firmly, so that every part of the veneer is brought in direct contact with the table-top, and any excess of glue is forced out at the edges. The work is then carefully laid aside to dry, after which it is trimmed up, cleaned and polished in the usual way.

For curved or angular work, the caul is made of an appropriate shape, and the clamps are increased, as it becomes necessary to multiply the points of pressure.

The press heretofore mentioned (see Tools and Implements) will prove extremely useful in veneering small work, serving the same purpose as the clamping bars, of which we give a sketch :

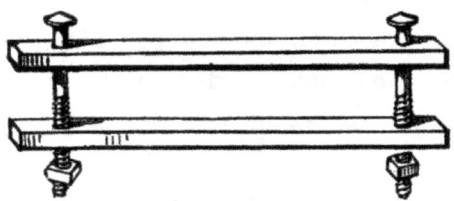

Ere we pass to another chapter and leave the subject of marquetry to the artizan's susceptibility of hints already given, we would suggest that the scope of this art adapts it for great variety. Not long since we inlaid a sign for a friend, who is a wood-engraver; and a black paper silhouette, which an itinerant skillful with scissors cut long ago, has been reproduced in wood many times, and gone among friends who appreciate it both for novelty and for memory's sake. Floors can be covered with appropriate patterns; walls and ceilings, door-panels, furniture, and in fact a multitude of articles that daily greet the eye, can be wrought with tasteful ornament and attractive device that will go far to prove the use of being clever.

CHAPTER VIII.

Gilding, Dyeing and Staining Woods.

For the information of those amateurs who believe that natural hues can be improved by human invention, we include this chapter. There are, however, times when circumstances demand such manipulation. White holly becomes of a more creamy tint by age. We have noticed the great beauty of this change, but the ubiquitous and unappreciative fly spared it not. Under such conditions the ornament may be stained black, by brushing it over, two or three times, with a strong decoction of logwood chips, and when it is dry, repeating the process with vinegar, in which old nails or iron-rust have been placed for a day or two. Common ink will do as a substitute for the vinegar preparation.

Other stains may be used, for the preparation of which we give some good recipes:

Purple Stain.

Logwood, 1 ounce; Brazil-wood, ¼ ounce; water, 1 quart. With these make a decoction, and stain the work therewith, after which the surface should be brushed over with a solution of a quarter-ounce of pearlash, dissolved in 1 quart of water. It produces a very beautiful and durable stain.

Red Stain.

Make a decoction of Brazil-wood, 2 ounces; potash, 2 ounces; water, 1 quart. Apply while hot, and afterward brush over with a solution of 2 ounces alum to 1 quart of water.

Light Mahogany Stain.

Madder, 2 ounces; fustic, 1 ounce; water, 1 quart. Boil until the decoction is complete. Having applied this to the work, wash it with a weak solution of potash.

Dark Mahogany Stain.

Proceed as for light stain, substituting half an ounce logwood for the madder.

Yellow Stain.

Furmeric, 1 ounce; spirits of wine, 1 pint. Allow it to stand until the former is extracted, when the tint will be ready for use.

All dyes or stains used for wood-work, should be made of such coloring matter as will leave a clear, bright finish. A dead hue must be strictly avoided, for there is no beauty where cheerfulness is lacking. Judgment should be exercised with every phase of fret-work. We must not stain or gild indiscriminately, lest the fashion of our handiwork seem tawdy and unnatural.

Gilding is an easy process, and occasionally applicable for touching up edges of brackets and a few other uses. The method is to affix gold-leaf by the aid of sizing, and, after it is well dried, burnishing the gilt with a smooth bit of agate, or else to procure a shell of gold from the artist's supply stores, and painting it upon the wood with a small camel-hair brush. It is quite seldom used, however, and even then sparingly.

Design for Clock Case.

CHAPTER IX.

Wood Carving.

Fret-sawing of itself is a study of outlines, the easy part of the work; and for further approach to completeness we must depend upon carving, success in which is attained by the aid of good sharp tools, natural tact, a steady hand, and patient love for the art. Civilization holds no monopoly for *whittling*. Columbus, during his first voyage across the Atlantic, discovered a rudely-carved staff floating on the waters, a specimen of aboriginal handiwork. The savage ornaments his war-club with strange device; the more enlightened artist gives meaning to his ornament, though often we meet with unintentional barbarism even in civilized efforts.

We spoke of "patient love for the art" as a requirement, the price of success. There is no speedier way to achieve it. Every little chip must be cut for a purpose, either to mar or to beautify the work, and he who is unwilling to tax his time and patience over each tiny line or depression, had best avoid carving. Capacity itself cannot be purchased; it is a result of industry, energy and will.

The tools we have already described, and we will now endeavor to

CARVED LETTER RACK.

render them useful and ready servants of our need. Tin swords are not adapted to cutting one's way through the world, and, though we may be redundant, we earnestly plead for the very best tools. Those imported from England are not yet excelled by any, Addis, the celebrated manufacturer, having won a well-deserved reputation.

Assuming that the requisite attention has been paid to sharp edges, and that the rough outlines of the frame here given have been cut with the scroll-saw, we will essay our skill in carving, in order to bring out the best effect.

Let us first study the leaves. At the extreme points they have a slight curvature, which, however, is not any higher than the wider portion. The diagram will explain this more plainly:

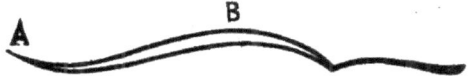

Now it will be obvious that the greatest (in fact, all) reduction of surface exists between A and B; therefore, with the chisel we begin hollowing it out, only gradually, for we must bear in mind that the surface of the leaf again slopes down to the edges, and it is far easier to cut away too little material, than to add any, when more than sufficient is detached. Expert carvers would use a gouge with somewhat flat edge for such work, but less practiced hands would find the skew-chisel a more convenient tool. The cutting should be done both ways from A and B, toward the centre of the depression, following the grain of the wood, as much as possible. With such work, it is not at all necessary to observe a mathematical exactness in the outline; a little irregularity adds to the effect, and prevents stiffness of appearance. This irregularity will be more requisite in carving this frame, because while the outer edges of the leaves are somewhat rounded, the edges which join the frame will require to be almost angular, in order to throw them more in relief.

The veining-tool must be used for marking the ribs, the larger one being made by cutting a double line from the stem, and gradually merging the two lines into one, as you work toward the end, and then the lateral or side ribs are to be formed of a single line joining the centre or mid-rib. These veins or ribs should not be cut deep, but distinct enough to show a clear, sharp line. The surface of the leaf can be neatly smoothed with the mezzotint-scraper, mentioned in a preceding chapter, and more convenient than sand-paper. The stem should be rounded, but left rough, in order to preserve a natural appearance, and the frame worked up in the same way; but as it is intended to be rustic, a series of fine lines should be cut upon its surface, to give it more roughness. The centre should be carved to match the rustic sides. Sand-paper should not be used at all for such work, and for the few occasions it may be necessary to use it, the carver will find it very convenient to whittle out slips of tough wood, somewhat in the shape of files, to which may be glued strips of sand-paper. A clear, clean cut with the tools will, in general, be quite sufficient. Whenever practicable, the work to be carved should be fastened firmly to a table, for both hands will be needed to operate the tools. To accomplish this, clamps of various sorts are used where the shape of the work will admit; the clamping-bars (spoken of under the head of Marquetry) may be employed to good advantage. An essential point is to have the work immoveable, except at the will of the carver. The tool should be guided by the larger fingers of the left hand, while it is pressed forward by the palm of the right hand upon the top or ball of the tool-handle. Thus the tool will acquire steadiness, and if the steel is good and the edge sharp, the cut will exhibit a corresponding smoothness.

Carving is a slow process, though so beautiful in results. It requires care and patience. The rules are few, and the art difficult to explain, practice illustrating it vastly better than precept. It is an old art; older, we are told, than sculpture or painting, and figures in the remote past, when Moses declared that God had " endowed Bezaleel and Aholiab with wisdom, knowledge and understanding to devise curious works in the carving of wood." We shall endeavor to give some plain and general directions, leaving to the judgment and intelligence of the carver, such variations and applications as a mechanical tact may indicate as demanded.

The outline or contour should be devoid of stiffness, and a graceful natural appearance preserved. Intersections of stems should be neatly worked out, by cutting away a portion of the wood, on each side of the under stem where the upper one crosses it. The depression must not be too abrupt, lest it seem like a dent made purposely, but the line of slope should be begun far enough back from the point of junction to allow a harmonious blending, and show a distinction between each stem.

Almost invariably the cutting should be *down*, and not *up;* away from, and not toward, the higher surfaces. This will be governed by the grain of the wood. Here we will repeat, that the material is strongest in the direction of the fibre, as we noticed in fret-sawing; and wherever we can maintain a good, strong purchase, it is best to render it available. Care should be observed that the surface is not splintered. No more force must be used, than sufficient to separate the chip, without detaching any adjacent fibre; in other words, the work is to be done altogether by *cutting*, and never by *rending*.

The carver must have complete command of his tools. He will sometimes find it expedient to use his chisel with the beveled end upward, which will sever only a thin shaving, as the direction of the edge is thus changed, and it is not able to enter the wood to as great a depth, and the chip is rather like the fine shaving made by a plane. By this simple plan, a great deal of curved work can be wrought more easily with a chisel than with a gouge.

The mezzotint-scraper, described already among the tools, will be found useful, in accordance with its name, for making smooth such surfaces as require its action, its shape adapting it to a various application. It is not in the quantity of tools, that true skill consists. Clever workmen will often do better work with one implement than others with twenty.

Like fret-sawing, wood-carving is capable of wide scope. Each is distinct of itself, yet susceptible of ready combination, like a chime of pleasant bells ringing many changes. The results of carving may be denominated "*petrified thought*," and we can well apply that saying of Roubiliac: "The figure is in the substance of the marble. I only extricate it from the enclosure or pick it out." Nature furnishes plenty of admirable models, the glorious handiwork of the Mighty Architect. In such a school, we can carefully study originals, fabricating their counterparts at our pleasure. The birds, the leaves, the flowers will serve as guides, and the nearer the reproduction, the better must be our skill. A knowledge of things as they are, and frequent reference to originals, will be necessary to an imagination that essays to copy nature; for if the work be a simple leaf, or a twig, nondescript deformities, unnatural bends, cannot escape ridicule. Judgment, perception and observation must direct, while the nimble fingers obey mechanically every behest of the brain.

Practice will discover various ways of application, and the chisel, wielded by a skillful hand, can exhibit a wonderful capability. In some of these pleasant paths we will wander.

A variety of figures can be cut out, as directed for overlay work, which being firmly glued to some flat surface, as a panel, may be wrought with the carving-tools, and appear to as good advantage as if carved from a solid piece. It would be less labor than to reduce the surface from around the ornament. Take heed, however, that the grain of both ornament and panel runs in the same direction. A cupboard may be thus decorated easily and with taste. The corners of doors may bear some pretty device, and the plainness which may in some cases "move more than eloquence," will be no less attractive for the tone of clever ornament. A few specimens will suffice to illustrate the hint; our space will hardly allow of extended description.

The labor-saving inventions of the present day have afforded us a cheap decoration in the *pressed-wood* ornaments that are now so

universally used for cabinet-work. American minds are too generally impatient to wait, and, therefore, are content to neglect the slower processes of old-fashioned art; but there are many productions of carving which cannot be *stamped out*. For the sake of the lazy ones, we will give some illustrations of the ready-made carvings. They are very well executed, low in price, and will serve as models for copying and practice.

The wood appears to receive its impress from a die acted upon by powerful force in the direction of the fibre.

CHAPTER X.

Overlaying.

The reverse of inlaying is overlaying, a process much more simple, yet quite as amenable to the principles of symmetry and taste. The design will stand in relief, or raised from the ground, and is often susceptible of further embellishment by means of the carving-tools.

For a simple instance, take the G already cut from the walnut wood, used for inlaying. If it be neatly cut and free from fractures, it presents as perfect an appearance as the holly inlay, though, on account of the bevel, it is the least bit smaller. From other pieces of walnut of the same thickness cut other letters of any similar style that may afford appropriate contrast, and enough in number to form an entire motto, as, " God Bless Our Home." It is not at all requisite to cut each letter separately, for you will observe there are three of O, one D, two of S, one L, two of E, and one each of U, B, R, H and M. This will involve cutting out ten times, or once for each letter. The most economical way is to cut three thicknesses at once, as the surplus letters will no doubt prove useful for other designs.

Having cut all the required letters, prepare also some lengths of neat bordering and four corner decorations, designs of which may be readily found among some of the pattern books. Now take a piece of white wood or pine, of ample size to furnish a back-ground for the motto, and cover it smoothly with good velveteen, velvet or cloth of some bright and cheerful color, attaching it to the wood, at the edges only, by means of glue or small tacks. The motto can then be neatly made upon it, with the letters, which, when correctly arranged, should be carefully glued fast. The border and ornaments can now be glued into their proper positions, taking care to lay them straight and equi-distant all around. Gilt or colored paper is sometimes used, but it has a tawdry, vulgar look, entirely unsuitable for handsome appearance. A neat bead-molding can then be framed around the work, and so a pleasing ornament will be accomplished.

Any of the silhouette designs can be treated in the same way, and a pretty conceit would be to decorate a sitting-room, with ornamental borders and other devices of one's own manufacture. Perhaps some enterprising publisher will, before long, think we have a full supply of frames, brackets, easels and such small wares, and then, it may be, patterns of window-cornices, lecterns and other useful articles will find a ready market among artizans who are at present looking in vain.

There is no reason why fret-sawing and wood-carving should not hold as familiar relations, with our homes, as fresco-painting, paper-hangings, or any other means of concealing unsightly places. We trust that all who follow the art, whether for profit or pleasure, will not be deterred from practising marquetry, because it is in any way more difficult than overlaying, and so be content with the easier work, for real merit sometimes consists of ability to perform what the occasion most demands.

We cannot forbear offering one or two designs, that may prove acceptable and useful, as we have found them. The first is a window-cornice, similar to one we made long ago, and the other design is one we drew, of a wooden mantle or chimney-piece:

These specimens can be produced by a tasteful combination of marquetry and overlaying. In the latter, the ornaments should, in addition to glueing, be fastened with tiny brads, and the whole surface well rubbed with glycerine or oil, to prevent it being warped by changes of temperature. Holly is scarcely appropriate for work so much exposed to dust, and some of the darker woods should be chosen. The cornice may be executed in marquetry, but it is our humble opinion that an overlay, of black walnut upon oak, would be more desirable to most people, as the relief would give more prominence to the ornaments, without being in the least obtrusive. The top-piece and braces, at the ends, should be of the same wood as the ground of the cornice, for, with them, the contrast of different colors would be too great. These pieces are to be cut separately, and afterward fastened in place, with brads and by glueing narrow cleats of wood, at the back, where they will not be seen. The finished structure can be fixed in place, over the window, by the usual iron braces or hooks.

For the same object, a continuous string of silhouettes may form the design; but there should be some relation between the several figures, lest the pattern seem a meaningless array of horses, dogs, men and all sorts of things, that look more like a Chinese puzzle than like a pure and simple piece of art.

The design of a mantle or chimney-piece, which we picture here, might excite the contempt of Holly and other writers upon decorative art, but even their phillipics against "jig-saw work" will scarcely satisfy the great majority of artizans, whose capital will not admit of the expense attendant upon solid carved work.

The ornaments can be varied to suit the taste, and may be overlaid, excepting the silhouette figures, *which must be inlaid.* The border, underneath the shelf, should be in relief, so as to break the stiffness of a direct line of junction between the shelf and the architrave or frieze. The ornaments of the side supports or jambs should be, at any rate, no thicker than the flat band at the edges, and we think it would appear to better advantage if these ornaments were not as thick as the band, so that a very flat look is avoided. This difference must be preserved, throughout, for all ornaments occupying similar positions, if adopted for any one. The main structure is joined together according to the usual methods of carpentry, and, as well-seasoned lumber is used, no trouble of springing or warping need be anticipated.

Owing to danger from fire, the middle portion, if grates are used, must be made of slate, marble or any other incombustible material, and encaustic tiles may be utilized for this purpose with beautiful effect.

Home, the shrine of our holiest, best emotions, may thus receive many an offering, replete with cheerful evidence of honest industry, the product of the labor we have loved.

Designs for Initials and Alphabets.

CHAPTER XI.

Cutting Out Work.

Tools that have no purpose, are as bad as hands with nothing to do. We propose to make our implements useful.

The hand-saw-frame requires all the steadiness obtainable. The tail of the frame should rest along the forearm, and against the shoulder if the frame is a long one, or under the shoulder if it be short; this will prevent the frame from swinging around and bending the saw-blade, and so causing it to cut crooked. The saw will actually dip or describe the arc of a circle as it passes through the wood, and this dip is reduced to the minimum by making short strokes instead of long ones.

Thus will plainly appear the great superiority of treadle-machines, which possess this steadiness in a greater degree, being fixed at those points where the support of the workman's arm and shoulder would be otherwise necessary, leaving both hands free to guide the work.

A great deal has been said about boring the saw-gates or holes for the entrance of the saw. It is our own experience, that a few general remarks are all that can safely be given, for the outlines of designs vary so much, that what would be true in one case might be false in another.

All the interior should be cut first, if possible, so that the surplus wood, around the outside, may serve as long as may be, for a continuous support to the more frail portions.

The illustration of a small frame given above, will serve as well as any other, to exemplify our meaning. We would begin this design at the top, boring the saw-gate near an angle, and cut in the direction of the line, till the angle is reached at the junction of the two curves. Now run the saw back a little more than its breadth, and turn it half-way around, and run it close down to the angle again. A very slight twist of the saw will now cause its cutting edge to catch upon the wood fibre as you begin to cut upon another line. Having reached the point at the top of the line, a slight sudden twist of the saw will cause its teeth to catch and follow yet another line. Backing the saw would be useless in such a case, as the angle is not acute enough to allow it to turn around. This rule will apply to all similar conditions.

If you observe the design carefully, you will notice that some of the lines run according to the grain of the wood, and such parts gain all the advantage of support from the grain, at every point where the fibre of wood is not severed or cut away, and wood is many times stronger on the line of its fibre than in any other direction.

You will further notice that other lines of the work run across the grain, especially the little projections or horns, on the outside edge of the frame. These being the weaker points, all the adjacent support, which they depend upon for the most of their strength, must not be removed too soon. If you cut the weaker portions first, whenever possible, you will decrease the support gradually, and, in like manner, diminish the danger of breaking. The outer edge of the design obtains an abundant support from the waste wood of the margin, which, at the same time, contributes somewhat to the strength of the interior portions; therefore, this waste wood should be cut away the very last of all.

The foregoing remarks are principles that will apply in every case. We have endeavored to be plain, even if we cannot be brief; so plain that the "wayfaring man, though a fool, shall not err therein." Perhaps mistakes may be more plenteous than success, while the learner gleans experience, step by step; but skill will surely be attained by carefully noting the points of stumbling.

Above all things, consideration must be shown for the frailty of the saw-blade, and the material should not be fed to it any faster than the teeth will cut. Our own treadle-machine has a foot attached, for holding work to the table, but we have never found it useful, the simple pressure of the fingers being all that is requisite for every purpose. The eye should be fixed upon the point where the saw-blade is operating, and follow the line, so that there shall be no deviation, for the mazy outlines will distract and puzzle the vision that wanders all over the design.

Thin sheets of metal, ivory, shell and very brittle material should be placed between thin layers of wood before being cut, as they would be apt to bend or break, even with the slight pressure of the saw-blade. By these means very delicate work can be wrought in composition-metal, silver, or even gold, appropriate for rich decoration, like the accompanying design on page 91, which would be suitable for the sides of a handsomely-bound book.

DESIGN FOR SIDE OF JEWEL BOX.

Design for Book Cover—Inlaid Work.

In the same manner, earrings and other jewelry may be produced from precious metals, of which we offer a neat design. Such elaborate work is worth a good treadle-machine:

We suggest metal as the proper material for such delicate work, as it possesses more tenacity than ivory or shell, and is, therefore, more durable. Any of these designs may be inlaid, as already described in the chapter on marquetry, or monograms can be worked with the precious metals in ivory or shell ornaments.

Let not fine lines deter you. If there is substance or strength enough to the material, the obedient saw will cut hair-lines as well as coarse ones, and the great beauty of fret-work is its exemption from all coarseness and heaviness.

You will notice some designs in this book, which may seem impossible of production to those who have never tried. They will be found useful in marquetry, the hair-lines being inlaid by cutting a channel for them with a saw of the same thickness as the lines, and then filling the interstice with thin shavings of wood. If neatly done, and it can be done easily, the effect will be very rich and elegant.

Design for Cover of Jewel Box.

Design for Mirror Frame.

CHAPTER XII.

BEVELING EDGES AND PUTTING WORK TOGETHER.

We knew once, a fret-sawyer who cut out a very handsome basket, but, from utter inability to put it together, was obliged to pay several dollars to a cabinet-maker for finishing the work. The fret-sawyer himself should complete what he begins, or at least be competent to do so. It is frequently requisite to join portions of work together, when the appearance of the joint is objectionable. To avoid this as much as possible, a knowledge of the relation of angles to each other must be acquired. By the following illustration of a hexagonal basket, you will observe, that if the sides were set up just as they are, they would meet each other only upon the inside edge, while on the outside quite a separation would appear; therefore, a proper angle must be made by sloping the inside edges sufficiently to make a close fit, and this is technically called *beveling* or mitring.

The method of determining the degrees of various angles, is exceedingly simple. In the case of this basket, measure the distance between the outside edges accurately, while the sides are held together in proper position. This will show the exact amount of beveling the pieces will require; but you must divide it equally between two sides of the basket, so that each may have an equal share. You will find a small pair of compasses convenient for determining the measurement; and then, calculating

the exact half, mark it off from the *inside* edges of each piece, when the surplus material can be cut off with the saw or shaved down with a sharp chisel.

This simple rule will apply to all work wherein a mitre is required, as glove-boxes and caskets, the sides of which should join each other at right angles. Such boxes are often lined with bright-colored silk or satin, which, if possible, should be first neatly fixed to pieces of cardboard of a size equal to the interior of the box, as it will be quite difficult to glue the silk directly to the wood without staining or wrinkling it.

There are other articles produced with the fret-saw which will require the practice of beveling, particularly clock-cases, one of which is here illustrated, because, in its construction, there are several of different angles:

The roof has one bevel; the two projecting pieces at the corners in front are beveled at the top, where they join the under side of the roof, and the sides and dial-piece have beveled edges, for fitting closely to the projections or abutments. These angles can all be easily determined in the same way as already described. Greater strength will be gained by glueing small bits of pine or other wood along the joints, inside of clock-cases; the interior being covered, such small blocks will not be seen.

Design for Picture Frame.

CHAPTER XIII.

The Warping of Wood.

Some woods which we have mentioned as addicted to the unpleasant habit of warping, will teach us the benefit of prevention, which may be often attained by storing the material in a dry place. The action of moisture upon the fibres, is to swell them unequally, so that one surface spreads, while the reverse does not change in the same degree, and this is the cause of the evil.

When the wood is not much warped, it will often straighten itself, if laid on the floor of a room that is not opened frequently. We have found this plan to work well on many occasions, but the wood must be removed as soon as it becomes straight, or it will warp and curl in the other direction. For very bad specimens, it will be most easy to steam the wood, by holding it over a kettle of boiling water, and, as it becomes straight, fasten it in the clamping-bars, mentioned under the chapter on Marquetry, until it becomes dry.

Well-seasoned wood is not very liable to warp, because it contains no sap, and the small amount of moisture in the atmosphere is scarcely enough to affect it seriously. When dry wood is warped, it may be straightened by heating on the side toward which it is to be set. It should be made quite hot, then set to shape, and retained in place until cold. A heavy piece will require to be heated, just short of coloring or charring. This process, if carefully performed, is superior to steaming, as the moisture is apt to raise the grain of the wood and make it look coarse. The object is to compress the grain on the side toward which it is set instead of expanding the reverse.

CHAPTER XIV.

Useful Hints.

The large field of operations to which fret-sawing belongs, and the various innumerable details that will present themselves to the amateur, call for a chapter wherein we can speak of matters unclassified, yet too useful to be forgotten. A really handsome piece of work can be easily spoiled in the fitting of it together.

Perhaps the subject of hinges is one of important interest. Such as are sold at the stores are quite simple and plain. We know of none whose ornamental character would commend them readily; but in view of their absence from the places of supply, we shall explain a means of obtaining them.

Sheet brass, copper, or other metals, can easily be procured, of various thicknesses. That best suited to our purpose, will range from 1-64 to 1-48 of an inch. Upon a piece of the requisite size, trace with a fine awl-point, any of the designs here given, and saw them out, according to the directions already given, leaving a flange sufficient to form a turn or socket, where the two parts of the hinge are united by the pin. At first, this flange will be straight, but by using small pliers, and working it, with light hammering, around a steel wire fully as large in diameter as the pin, until it forms a tubular shape, its use will be quite plain. To the other half of the hinge, there will be, of course, two of these flanges to be treated in like manner. The pin should be fitted as true as possible, the centre flange having ease to work upon it, for if it fits tightly, it will be useless.

Sometimes, the ornamental portion can be neatly soldered to the ordinary square hinges, but with practice it is much more easy to form the joints on the work. A little filing may be requisite to clean up corners and edges. Such hinges should be fastened on with small wire pins, holes of proper size being drilled through the metal and wood. The pins should be cut off almost flush, on th under side, and a few light taps of a small hammer will rivet them sufficient to hold firmly.

Similar fixtures may be contrived to answer the purpose of

catches or locks. The use of them has been so limited heretofore, that they have been quite difficult to procure. The skillful amateur can manufacture them himself, according to his own fancy as to pattern or shape. We illustrate a few styles:

These catches are fastened to one door of a cabinet, by means of a small brass pin. On the border of the opposite door is set a small round-headed brass screw, the head of which is flattened to pass through the slot in the catch. The screw-head being then turned to the opposite direction, the doors are fastened, at will.

We suppose it is generally known that the wire pins and loops of brooches, earrings or other jewelry are not all gold, though they glitter; otherwise they would not have enough *spring* or elasticity to be serviceable. They are simply a wire of some baser metal, composition or brass, plated with gold enough to prevent corrosion. The wire may be purchased by weight, or the fixtures, already made, by the pair, at the stores where jewelers' supplies are sold. The latter is probably the cheapest way to purchase. They are not expensive.

There are many other small fixtures, such as metal loops, wherewith to suspend clock-cases, frames and such articles in their proper places. For these, sheet brass is applicable, and symmetric form may be given by aid of the scroll-saw, either ornamental or plain, as the taste may dictate. As nail-heads vary in size, the hole by which the loop is passed over the nail should be sufficiently roomy for the largest-sized picture-nail, if the width of the brass plate will admit it.

Corner braces will often prove of additional advantage for fret-work boxes. These may be cut from metal, in pairs, by following the directions given in a preceding chapter, fastening the thin sheets of metal between layers of wood. If the expense is not an objection, these braces may be nickel-plated, at small cost.

Appropriate feet for the bottoms of boxes and other articles that are designed to stand upon a shelf or table, may be made of large glass beads, uniform in size, being fastened to the wood by a thin screw passed through the hole in the centre of the bead. If the screw fits snugly, the head of it may be cut off with a file, so that no part of it shall project from the outside of the bead. An atom of any good cement will oftentimes hold the shank of the screw firmly. Fancy brass-headed upholsterers' nails are also very convenient for a like purpose.

CHAPTER XV.

PLEASURE AND PROFIT.

Of the pleasure incident to pretty homes, we need not preach a long sermon. It is becoming so fixed upon the minds and the hearts of the people, that home decoration seems less an adjunct than an essential of our being. . The pictures of dearly loved ones, far distant, perhaps gone to a quiet rest beneath the sod, are none the less valued because of the chaste enshrinement of frames. There is "*an everlasting fitness of things*," which demands this ornament, and it is a part of home, just as much as anything else. Education and refinement demand it as a witness of their existence. As well might we question the utility of the lily or the rose, as to deny the mission of taste and pleasant adornment, in the place where all our highest and holiest emotions concentrate. Remembering that it has become so universally recognized, we feel that the subject stands in need of no further commendation. The text that we have read a thousand times, seems ever new, when the brilliant colors of illumination render it attractive to the eye, and after the art of fret-work or carving has rendered it a thing of rarer beauty, we suspend it where we can gaze upon it, and pray from our inmost souls:

GOD BLESS OUR HOME.

And, moreover, we appreciate those things which have a history. It is not enough that they have a value of dollars and cents. Memory gives them a higher worth, because of the hand that has labored for our sakes in many a token of affection.

There is another phase to the pleasure of this art. It serves to discipline the mind, and fill up gaps in our leisure hours, by affording an instructive recreation. We become better acquainted with things around us, for we seek our originals among them, oftentimes. We shall wonder at the immeasurable Wisdom which gave the woods of the forests quite as distinctive tints as the flowers of the meadow, and the curious mind will be led to wander in pleasant paths of investigation and knowledge. The olive shall remind of that matchless Sermon on the Mount, which is ever entertaining to us. The mahogany will tell us a story of that courtly navigator, Raleigh, mending his ships on the coast of a new-found country, and the mass of information will accumulate, till we find there is much that we yet can learn.

Aside from the benefits of instruction already declared, the art we treat of has other aims and purposes. Its practice induces attention to detail which characterizes perfect work, fully as valuable as drawing, painting and kindred arts. We could cite even more support in its favor, but will not occupy your patience further than to say that fret-sawing and wood-carving would serve a purpose sufficiently noble, if it only furnished something for idle hands to do; and so we pass on to consider the profitable part of the question.

We speak from positive experience of such cases, a few among so many which we know of and can produce, and can say, without reservation, that fret-sawing, faithfully done, is as remunerative an employment as many other callings. Poor work is dear at any price. The cases we will cite were those characterized by neat, careful labor, not at all difficult to perform, and, in fact, what some older amateurs would consider rudimental.

One young man we know of, who found it impossible to obtain employment at any mercantile pursuit, became possessed of a foot-power scroll-saw, and by its aid, produced brackets, card-baskets, match-boxes, frames and other articles, to give him, when sold, a clear profit of five dollars per day. Hundreds of others have earned from fifty to seventy-five dollars each, by the sale of work done at leisure times. For five years, fret-work has been regularly exhibited at the annual fairs, throughout the Eastern States; it has one weekly publication devoted almost entirely to its interest; about a dozen different parties are engaged in printing designs, exclusively as a business, and more than thirty thousand foot-power scroll-saws have been manufactured and sold to parties who are now using them for pleasure or for profit. Beyond that number are all those who use the ordinary hand-saw, probably three times as many more. We have long ago earned all the cost of machine, saws, attachments and all the parapharnalia, without confinement to the art as a means of profit, for friends were numerous, and we gave away ten times as many as we sold. From a square foot of black walnut, we have made, in a few hours, a beautiful clock-case, worth at least five dollars, the material costing ten cents. A piece of ebony, worth about one cent, furnished enough material for a handsome cross, for which one person would have gladly given a couple of dollars. A square foot of good black walnut will be sufficient to make four or five pretty brackets, or more than twice as many match-cases, which will readily sell for upwards of fifty cents each. Allowing twenty cents for material and pattern, the net profit for about half a day's work would pay for one-sixth of the cost of the best foot-power scroll-saw made, with all the extra attachments. Many of these scroll-saws found their way to foreign countries during the Centennial Exhibition of last year, and they are still being sent thither, where their use will continue to give them a warm welcome among artizans, amateurs and others, who will appreciate them more and more.

The reader will find many fine designs in this volume, which require but little material to execute. The cornice of which we have given an illustration (page 83) need not cost one dollar, over and above what the labor may be worth, and any one can judge the value of such a fine window decoration. So we might continue enumerating instances of profit in the practice of this art.

With little to guide us save the course of the tiny saw-blade, working its way through the mazy plan before us, we have written thus much to present the subject plainly to beginners, and with a spirit of fraternal good-will to those amateurs who have achieved, by patient practice, a high degree of excellence. If it has served its purpose, as intended, of a compendium of practical information, perhaps it may be deemed a pleasure as well as a profit to many.

DESIGN IN SILHOUETTE—THE START AND THE RETURN.

ENVOI.

Through a pleasant maze of delicate tracery and friendly chatting over pretty things that make home bright and cheerful, we bring our book to a close, and go back again to the workshop, where the fret-saw waits to do our bidding, in the execution of yet greater attempts. We are no more content with being an average fret-sawyer than to be an average man, but take delight in weaving gossamer threads into fairy forms, till we reach the full complement of possibility. In the pursuit of this higher region of **Art**, we ask your pleasant company and good wishes, and a rivalry of honest workers, undismayed by intricate design or test of patience. And so for a while, Adieu!

INDEX.

		PAGE
INTRODUCTION,		5
CHAPTER I.	OF MATERIALS,	7
" II.	OF SAWS, SAW FRAMES AND TREADLE MACHINES,	21
" III.	OTHER TOOLS AND IMPLEMENTS,	37
" IV.	OIL STONES, ETC.,	45
" V.	OF GLUE, POLISH, SAND PAPER, PASTE, ETC.,	49
" VI.	OF DESIGNS,	53
" VII.	OF MARQUETRY,	57
" VIII.	GILDING, DYEING AND STAINING WOODS,	69
" IX.	WOOD CARVING,	73
" X.	OVERLAYING,	81
" XI.	CUTTING OUT WORK,	87
" XII.	BEVELING EDGES AND PUTTING WORK TOGETHER,	95
" XIII.	THE WARPING OF WOOD,	99
" XIV.	USEFUL HINTS,	101
" XV.	PLEASURE AND PROFIT,	105
	ENVOI,	110

DESIGNS CONTRIBUTED.

PAGE 4.	PICTURE FRAME,	By Trump Bros.
" 20.	CROSS,	By J. T. Pratt & Co.
" 36.	WALL POCKET,	" " "
" 44.	BRACKET IN LEAF WORK,	Williams' Designs.
" 48.	CROSS,	By J. T. Pratt & Co.
" 56.	MARQUETRY DESIGN,	Williams' Designs.
" 72.	CLOCK CASE,	By T. F. Washbourne.
" 86.	INITIALS,	Williams' Designs.
" 91.	BOOK COVER,	" "
" 93.	JEWEL BOX,	" "
" 94.	MIRROR FRAME,	" "
" 98.	PICTURE FRAME,	" "
" 109.	SILHOUETTE,	German of Konewka.
" 112.	SILHOUETTE,	" "

DESIGN IN SILHOUETTE.

www.ingramcontent.com/pod-product-compliance
Lightning Source LLC
Chambersburg PA
CBHW060424010526
44118CB00017B/2353